Dear Reader:

The book you are about to read is the latest bestseller from the St. Martin's True Crime Library, the imprint *The New York Times* calls "the leader in true crime!" Each month, we offer you a fascinating account of the latest, most sensational crime that has captured the national attention. St. Martin's is the publisher of bestselling true crime author and crime journalist Kieran Crowley, who explores the dark, deadly links between a prominent Manhattan surgeon and the disappearance of his wife fifteen years earlier in THE SURGEON'S WIFE. Suzy Spencer's BREAKING POINT guides readers through the tortuous twists and turns in the case of Andrea Yates, the Houston mother who drowned her five young children in the family's bathtub. In Edgar Award-nominated DARK DREAMS, legendary FBI profiler Roy Hazelwood and bestselling crime author Stephen G. Michaud shine light on the inner workings of America's most violent and depraved murderers. In the book you now hold, EVERY WOMAN'S NIGHTMARE, investigative journalist Steven Long tells the harrowing truth behind the disappearance and murder of Lori Hacking, a story that rocked Utah and the nation.

St. Martin's True Crime Library gives you the stories behind the headlines. Our authors take you right to the scene of the crime and into the minds of the most notorious murderers to show you what really makes them tick. St. Martin's True Crime Library paperbacks are better than the most terrifying thriller, because it's all true! The next time you want a crackling good read, make sure it's got the St. Martin's True Crime Library logo on the spine—you'll be up all night!

Charles E. Spicer, Jr.
Executive Editor, St. Martin's True Crime Library

St. Martin's

True Crime Library Titles

by Steven Long

Out of Control

EVERY WOMAN'S NIGHTMARE

The True Story
of the Fairy-Tale Marriage
and Brutal Murder
of Lori Hacking

STEVEN LONG

St. Martin's Paperbacks

EVERY WOMAN'S NIGHTMARE

Copyright © 2006 by Steven Long.

Cover photo of couple courtesy Soares and Hacking families/ZUMA Press. Mugshot courtesy Salt Lake County jail.

ISBN: 0-312-93741-5
EAN: 9780312-93741-6

Printed in the United States of America

St. Martin's Paperbacks edition / April 2006

St. Martin's Paperbacks are published by St. Martin's Press, 175 Fifth Avenue, New York, NY 10010.

10 9 8 7 6 5 4 3 2 1

For Lloyd and Gailyn

For Everything

Acknowledgments

The making of a book is much like running the Ironman. You do it alone, and along the way many obstacles, walls if you will, are thrown up to prevent a successful finish. Yet in any marathon there are caregivers along the way offering help to get you to the end. Such are the people who make successful authorship possible. That is why we write acknowledgments as a way of saying thank you.

First thanks go to Dr. Pricilla Ray of the Texas Medical Center whose advice was immeasurable. We have all heard the term "pathological liar." Yet understanding such a person, and digesting the narcissistic personality disorder that provokes such behavior requires knowledge beyond my capabilities. I couldn't have been the beneficiary of such expertise without the help of my friend Tom Sartwelle, an attorney who has always been generous with a piece of advice and ready good humor. He is a truly great pal. A special thank you must go to my old friend Vicki Saito of the Duke University School of Medicine.

Many in Utah helped in ways deserving something

beyond a mere thank you in the front of a book. Unfortunately, they have asked to remain anonymous. Suffice it to say that I will be forever grateful for their time, good counsel, a bed to sleep in, and the sharing of a wonderful bottle of red wine at the end of the day. They gave me an insider's insight into the working of America's "Beehive State."

There are those in Utah whom I can name. Reverend Ron Belnap is a retired Episcopal priest who grew up Mormon. He was married in the Salt Lake Temple, as was his wonderful wife, Nancy. They opened their home and their hearts to me, and provided a firm foundation on which my understanding of the faith of Latter-day Saints is built.

Writing true crime books necessitates a working relationship with the lawyers and cops involved in a case. Often, prosecutors are standoffish and obtuse. This was not true of Bob Stott of the Salt Lake County DA's Office. Working with police can be difficult for a journalist. There is usually a mutual distrust on both ends that sometimes is impossible to overcome. Such was not the case with the Salt Lake City Police Department. In particular, I want to thank Detectives Phil Eslinger, Dwayne Baird, and J. R. Nelson. The department is among the best in the nation. The citizens of Zion rest comfortably in the knowledge that they are under the watchful eye of such consummate professionals in law enforcement.

In particular I want to thank the Salt Lake City–based journalists who spilled their sweat and spent sleepless nights covering the story of the disappearance of Lori Hacking and her murder. They did the heavy lifting. Zion's reporters have been generous in giving their time to me. I have relied upon their clips for this book when no other source was available. In particular, kudos go out to the staffs of the Associated Press, the *Deseret Morning News, The Salt Lake Tribune*, KSL radio and television, and KUTV for their consummately professional work.

The final draft could not have come to fruition without the unselfish help of those who proofread my work. Special thanks go out to my wife, Vicki, who is truly my partner in everything, and to Roni Nordquist, Gailyn Smith, and Brenda Greene.

This book could not have been produced in its present state without the unselfish help of Paul Soares, the victim's older brother. He provided me a glimpse into the world of his and Lori's wonderful and accomplished family. He also helped invaluably in my understanding of Mark Hacking. Your graciousness will be long remembered.

As always, special thanks also to my longtime literary agent Jane Dystel in New York, as well as the best editors I could have dared asked for, Charles Spicer and Joe Cleemann, of St. Martin's Press.

Finally an author's hugs go to our friend Vicki Bell for just being there in times of need. There will be a special place in heaven just for you.

October 2005
Houston

EVERY
WOMAN'S
NIGHTMARE

Chapter One

"I believe that I am a child of God, endowed with a divine birthright. I believe that there is something of divinity within me and within each of you. I believe that we have a Godly inheritance and that it is our responsibility, our obligation, and our opportunity to cultivate and nurture the very best of these qualities within us."

—Gordon B. Hinckley, President, Prophet, Seer, and
Revelator of The Church of Jesus Christ of Latter-day Saints
(Brigham Young University, 1992)

Summer 2004

SALT LAKE CITY—The elder pointed the gun in anger, anger like none he had ever felt. He looked at her full head of hair. In Texas, they would call it big hair. But this wasn't Texas. This was Utah, where women wore big hair, and complemented the coiffure with the best makeup their money could buy. The bullet lay in the chamber, lethal lead an eighth of an inch in diameter and a quarter inch in length. It was designed for killing small game—rabbits, birds, squirrels, and an occasional reptile. But it was a favorite of street thugs as well, when loaded in a Saturday night special. The load waited to do its deadly work.

The elder was in command, as always. A god walking on his own personal planet, the world was his. He had been groomed from birth to maintain absolute command of his home. He looked at her sleeping, thinking of how she had betrayed him. She had no right to question his motives or the world that he had created for himself and those around him. Yet she had challenged him, and if she wasn't stopped, she would soon betray him to the people he cared for most, the very people he had spent a lifetime wanting desperately to please.

The anger was palpable. He had worked so hard to create his world, even though he knew that it was a façade. She had destroyed it as surely as if she had stepped on a roach. He had planned his life so carefully, crafting a perfect lie, a fairy tale that could never be. Tonight, she had killed him with words, without knowing the brutality of her act. The anger was bitter in his mouth as he lowered the gun toward her luxuriant head of hair. Beneath it the pillowcase was still wet from Lori's tears.

> ELOHIM: We will put the sisters under covenant to obey the law of Obedience to their husbands. Sisters, arise. Each of you bring your right arm to the square. You and each of you solemnly covenant and promise before God, angels, and these witnesses at this altar that you will each observe and keep the law of your husbands, and abide by his counsel in righteousness. Each of you bow your head and say "Yes."

—The Law of Obedience, Mormon Endowment Ceremony as
it was until 1990 when it was softened somewhat.

Their August 1999 marriage in the Temple in Bountiful had been perfect, the ultimate culmination of love, the joining of two childhood sweethearts. There in the gleaming white building, its spire soaring high above greater Salt Lake City and in view of the Great Salt Lake itself, the two were wed in a traditional Mormon wedding, tiny by the standards of other Christian sects.

Each had donned temple garments covering the body, neck to ankles and wrists, worn only by the best Mormons deemed to be "Temple worthy," having passed tests imposed to determine their righteousness.

They had performed their endowment, and had been washed and anointed after removing all of their clothing, each by an "officiator" of the same sex who laid hands on their heads and pronounced a formula. Each then entered a booth and received the washing, or a token wetting of each part of the body with a blessing that the part function properly. Each part, the head, eyes, nose, neck, shoulders, arms, legs, feet, and loins are blessed. At the end of the rite, the officiators again placed hands upon their heads and uttered a short prayer sealing the washing, and cleansing each from the "sins of this generation."

Then the entire ritual was repeated with each body part being touched with olive oil.

It was then that Mark and Lori were clothed in the simple white garments of the Holy Priesthood that they had brought with them. On the garment, symbols were sewn at the right knee, the navel, and over each nipple.

From childhood they had been taught that selecting their life's mate was perhaps the most important thing that they would ever do, since marriage was sealed "for time and all eternity." Thus it was that Lori would be bound to Mark, not only in this life, but in the next as well. A church tradition suggests that they had selected their mate in their prior existence before coming to earth.

Inside the huge stone walls the families had gathered, faithful to their religion, all dressed in their Temple garments for the occasion, steadfast in their beliefs, certain that the simple garments under their clothes afforded them protection.

The sealing ceremony was brief. Dressed in a white suit, the officiator told the couple to kneel at the altar and face each other, joining hands in the special and secret Mormon patriarchal grip. Then simple vows were exchanged and the two were pronounced husband and wife. Stark by the standards of other Christian sects, there are no flowers, no music, no poetry, and the father doesn't give the bride away. Moreover, the exchange of wedding rings is not a part of the ceremony, and is optional.

In gleaming white, the Temple housed Bountiful's most sacred places, space reserved for the anointed—truly anointed—of the Mormon faith. There the Soareses and the Hackings had gathered for the wedding of Mark and Lori, both in communion with their faith.

There was no "Dearly Beloved, we are gathered . . ." There was no vast sanctuary filled to the brim with friends and family. Instead, a handful of those closest to the couple joined them in the small "Sealing Room" of the Temple which looked much more like a hotel lobby than a church. Only the Temple worthy were allowed to attend, and those left behind must wait outside, or in a waiting room set aside for the as-yet unworthy.

For spiritually inclined Mormon girls (*women* is not a word used often in this faith for the young unmarried female) this was the key to eternity. Quite simply, according to the faith, unmarried women can never enter paradise unless they are at the side of a man. As such, marriage for Mormon women is considered essential to attain the highest spiritual state after death, the Celestial Kingdom. Tiny Lori Soares was such a woman. Moreover, she knew that she was destined to spend that eternity at the side of Mark, such was the depth and confidence of her love for him.

When the time came, Lori could count on eternity at the side of Mark. Her unmarried sisters would have the bad fortune of never attaining the Latter-day Saint equivalent of Heaven.

Mark Hacking carried his tiny bride across the threshold of their new apartment filled with the expectation of a long and wonderful life together. He adored Lori, and had since he was 14. Now she was his and the two would stroll arm and arm into the Celestial Kingdom as their reward for a good life lived in the faith. With luck, they would be joined by a brood of Hackings of their making.

A string of pleasant surprises greeted Lori during her first encounter living with a man. The horror stories she had heard from her married girlfriends and relatives, or imagined from a lifetime of watching television, just weren't true about Mark.

There were no dirty socks lying in the corner of the bedroom where he'd shed them. There was no dirty or soiled underwear thrown haphazardly across the bed or at the foot of the dresser. In the kitchen, dishes covered with an unfinished meal weren't left in the sink, but were washed as soon as the table was cleared. Snack food wrappers weren't strewn around chairs that Mark had sat in. Mark was tidy to a fault.

Living with Mark was fun at first, a prolonged honeymoon. Yet little things did get to her. Sometimes she caught him in white lies, innocent yet annoying.

The two had spent a delightful honeymoon in Las Vegas. When Mark and Lori returned to Salt Lake City, it was to Mark's two-bedroom apartment on Lincoln Street.

Mark had secured a job, and the apartment, a couple of months before. He signed on as manager of the small complex, getting free rent in the bargain. It was an ideal situation for two newlyweds starting life on a limited budget with the male of the family a full-time student soon destined for more long years in medical school and a residency.

Lori fell into the routine of being a resident manager of the seven Lincoln Street apartments. Tenants moved in, tenants moved out. It wasn't the kind of complex that had a large maintenance staff. She and Mark were it. If a swamp cooler (a kind of air conditioner used in Western states) was on the blink, it was up to Mark to fix it. When a vacancy occurred, the couple made the apartment like new again for the next tenant, including completely re-painting the interior if need be. Lori joined in with exuberance.

"It was funny," her brother Paul recalled. "Lori had never done anything like that."

When they opened their front door, the two of them walked into a cookie cutter apartment.

The floor plan was simple, much like a jillion starter apartments across the nation. It was an oblong box with thin partitions as walls erected to create the privacy of rooms. Once inside the apartment's door, a small kitchen was the first thing a visitor would see. A bar, a standard architectural trick used to make the entire space appear larger, separated the kitchen and the living room. On the opposite wall, each of the two bedrooms' doors opened independently. A small common bath separated them. The master bedroom was on the right.

In the living room, pictures hung on the wall, common decorator items picked up in a home furnishing store—or perhaps at a garage sale. The couple's TV sat on a stand outside the door to their bedroom. On the other side, a small table housed Mark's Nintendo when it wasn't in use, which was infrequent when he was at home.

The apartment had limited seating, with only a recliner, sofa and love seat for the couple and their guests. Shortly before their marriage Lori had come into the sofa when a former roommate moved and was unable to take it with her.

Occasionally the house would fill with out-of-town guests, some staying overnight. During family gatherings, the women would crowd into the tiny apartment kitchen to prepare meals and snacks. At one such gathering, Jana, Lori's stepmom, and Eli, her half-sister, were caught on video having a great time. The scene would later become famous as it was repeated again and again on news shows and cable programs, many mistaking the tape for a party hosted by Lori's friends immediately before her death.

On a few occasions, the sofa also served as a bed for Lori's brother Paul when he came to town.

"When I would go to Utah we would mostly see them at night and meet them at the apartment and go out to dinner or something like that," he later remembered.

Paul found talking to Mark particularly stimulating. "I never thought of him as a shallow person. His conversations and concerns for people were genuine," he remembered.

"Mark was very liberal in his point of view," Paul says. "I don't know if he was registered as a Democrat or a Republican, but his viewpoints were very liberal. I remember when Mark was down at my mom's house for the fourth of July. We were discussing the gay marriage issue, and Mark was saying how much he was in favor of it. Lori was more conservative, but Mark was very liberal."

Conversations with Mark often turned to trivia. "He was really into those worthless facts-of-knowledge things and loved doing crossword puzzles."

After Paul's divorce in his first marriage, he found solace in his sister, coming back to Salt Lake City and crashing on the sofa late one night at Mark and Lori's apartment.

"That was one of my most special memories with Lori, because I had just gotten divorced and Lori and I had time to really talk about things," he said.

Scattered around the apartment, family photos gave testimony to the closeness of the large Hacking brood, as well as to Lori's smaller but equally close family, at the center of them, Mark and Lori, a happy, well-adjusted young couple exuding confidence.

Their place made a statement: An apartment's furnishings don't need to be expensive to deliver a sense of taste and style. Their two-bedroom apartment had both.

"Lori was good at that type of stuff," her brother Paul remembered.

The couple was busy—busy all the time. When he wasn't in school, Mark was in the outdoors cultivating his lifelong passion for the mountains. Lori was much more an indoor type. Most recently she had taken up the fad of scrapbooking that had swept the nation to the point that franchise stores had sprung up in strip centers from Maine to California.

The small-town girl from Orem loved living in the city at the thick of things near downtown. The apartment sat just down the street from Temple Square itself, the epicenter of Mormon Utah, and a stone's throw from the ornate state capitol building.

Whenever she could, she would catch a movie or play. When the opportunity presented itself, Lori and her mom would go to the Mormon Tabernacle to hear its world-famous choir. That was special to Lori because she knew how much her mother loved music, and how much a part of her life it had become.

And there were always those special nights when she just went out to dinner with her girlfriends. It was a habit begun in high school when she and her chums would buzz into a fast-food joint for a burger or shake. As an adult, it had evolved into evenings sitting at a restaurant with white tablecloths.

Lori was also active in the Relief Society at her church. Devout Mormon women joined the group to do good works. Critics across Utah claimed the Relief Society's major work was relieving overburdened women of the gossip they had bottled up inside that was bursting to get out and be told.

Mark was active in the Church as well, but his devotion was largely for appearances.

He was determined to get Lori outdoors. Mark began jogging, and soon his wife joined him, as much to humor her new husband as to stay in shape. It wasn't long until the couple was entering 10K runs—several of them.

Mark and Lori sometimes walked the short distance to City Creek Canyon and launched a jog from its entrance near Memory Grove. Both became health-conscious, eating non-fattening foods and salads. And despite the pure mountain water of Salt Lake City, Mark was convinced that the couple needed a water purifier. He constantly had to fill it.

The two settled into a routine. Lori would go to work and Mark would go to school. They didn't see much of each other during the week except for the occasions when Lori slipped away from work to catch a quick lunch with her husband on campus. She would drive up, and Mark, toting a backpack full of books, would meet her between classes for a quick sandwich on the run.

To all appearances, the marriage of Mark and Lori Hacking was perfect.

His mind was racing as he stood by the bed in 127 South Lincoln, Apartment 7. She looked relaxed, no longer the hellcat who had confronted him not so long ago.

The blowup had been extreme.

It had begun when they got home from a party thrown by Lori's work friends as a going-away send-off. As soon as they left, she'd started in on him, saying vicious things to him, and then belittling him in his own home. In situations such as this, Lori could be formidable, her superior intellect meshing with her temperament.

Her friends always called her a spitfire. *Little did they know,* Mark thought. For a Mormon man, there was no greater insult from a woman, any woman. To insult him in his own home, to challenge him the way she had challenged him, was unthinkable.

Lori had known her place in this world since childhood, but this night she had violated it.

Lori stared her husband down and bluntly called him a liar, destroying his manhood again and again as she confronted Mark about the untruths she had discovered.

That Friday, Lori had phoned Randee Alston at the University of North Carolina, inquiring about financial aid. Alston had checked several different databases before telling Lori that Mark was not registered at the school, and had never even submitted an application. Mark had tried to sidestep the situation with a story that he'd phoned Alston and been told that it was a misunderstanding caused by a computer malfunction, but the truth had come out at last.

Lori told Mark that she was sick of his lies. Worse still for him, she told her husband that he had to leave.

Lori had kept the secret of troubles in the marriage quiet for too long, covering up the fact that Mark Hacking was what most would call a pathological liar. During the last year or so, she had begun to tell a handful of friends that her marriage was troubled. For most, though, she maintained the façade of the perfect Mormon marriage. There was only so much of Mark's deception that she could handle, and this was the biggest lie of them all.

She had quit her job, a job she loved, and was pulling up stakes and moving across a continent for him, only to discover that it was all an elaborate ruse, manufactured to make Mark appear to be more of a hero, more of a man, more of a Hacking than he in fact was.

How could he dare to create something so gigantic in its deception, so daring a lie? He had outdone himself, she shrieked.

Mark's intellect was no match for his wife's, and he could only stand there and take it as she continued her relentless assault, attacking his ego and thereby attacking his manhood itself.

It wasn't enough that she was winning the fight with her tiny hands tied behind her back; she was doing it with blunt verbal stabs punctuated by the biting sarcasm that had made her such a delight to be around in social situations.

The two were going to have a baby together, and Lori told her husband that the child would likely grow up without the benefit of a nuclear family—without a father in the house. The statement cut her to the core, but it had to be made, because with his latest shenanigan, Mark Hacking had driven Lori to the edge, to the thing any Mormon wife dreads the most, the destruction of the family unit.

Mormonism's great strength is that its very foundation is made up of families tied to the Church through common beliefs and common needs. Now, Mark had destroyed the possibility of that.

Lori could not, would not, explain this away to her family, to the Hackings, or to the couple's friends. How could she?

The embarrassment of such a preposterous lie being foisted upon her!

How could Mark do this to her? she asked him. He stood before her, mute.

"Let's go to the store and get something to drink," was the best he could muster.

"And when we get back, you start packing," she answered, venom in her voice.

When they returned, Lori had even taken the time to write a letter to Mark before she went to bed, too tired to speak any longer.

The letter was folded. On its outside, simply "Mark." She was telling him that he had to change.

"I want to grow old with you, but I can't do it under

these conditions . . . I can't imagine life with you if things don't change," she wrote. "I hate coming home from work because it hurts to be home in our apartment."

The letter indicated that the problems with Mark had been growing quietly inside Lori as she presented the perfect façade of their marriage to the outside world. Lori, at least when she wrote the letter, was thinking the unthinkable for a Mormon woman. She was contemplating divorce.

"I can't imagine life with you if things don't change," she wrote, the words cutting Mark to the quick as he read them.

Lori was a winner, and she wanted to be married to a winner as well. She had now come to the realization that she had committed to someone altogether different from her.

"I got someone I don't want to spend the rest of my life with unless changes are made," she told her husband in the unarguable format of the handwritten page.

His story of graduating with honors from the University of Utah in May was undone. She now knew that he hadn't attended classes in two years. Worse, she now also knew that he had not been accepted to the University of North Carolina School of Medicine.

These were the lies he'd told her—and their families and friends.

The ruse had been so complex, so complete. In two days, his father would take leave of his thriving medical practice to go with Mark and Lori to North Carolina and help get the couple settled into the life of a freshman medical student and his wife.

Doug Hacking was so proud that another son would become a doctor, a bold measure of success by any standard.

Mark had no doubt he could fool his father into believing that he was to attend medical school during the trip North Carolina. He had grown up in a medical environment. He knew all the jargon that his father could throw at him. He could walk the walk and talk the talk. Mark Hacking knew that he wouldn't be caught, that he would be able to pull off the long trip without a hitch.

After all, Mark had fooled his childhood pal Ross Williams, now a Utah probation officer. The two had been buddies since pre-school. Recently, they had talked about the difference in cost between living in Utah and living in Chapel Hill. Ross believed every word he had been told.

Mark held the letter in his hand, fury welling inside of him.

How dare she? How dare she tell him anything? It was her place to stand beside him, unquestioning, obedient, and righteous. It was her place to bear the burdens of childbirth, maintain a comfortable home, and in general live for him, enduring his likes and dislikes, forgiving his foibles at worst, and reveling in them at best.

Much of their world was steeped in the 1950s, an *Ozzie and Harriet* universe.

A woman's place was in the home, and the women of the state knew it.

Lori clearly didn't know her place.

Still clutching the gun, Mark the elder stood looking at her, his anger mounting. The curls of her hair against

the pillow were beautiful despite his anger. Her puck-
ish chiseled Latin face was now softened in sleep, her
anger lapsed into unconsciousness. Yet Mark did not
feel warmth for Lori any longer. Their marriage had
become a competition, and she had become another in
a long list of obstacles to him, another of a long list of
overachievers who eclipsed him.

Marriage to Lori had become a habit, and a bad
one at that. He should have known she would betray
his secret if she ever unraveled it. Women were so
unstable, so unreliable, so emotional. They certainly
couldn't be trusted with secrets like his, he mused. She
had bought his lies, just as they all had. Yet she was the
ultimate stakeholder. Soon, very soon, the two were to
have left for a new life on the East Coast. Now it had
come to this, he thought, his hand gripping the gun
fiercely in his anger.

> "I know that there are transgressors, who, if they knew
> themselves and the only condition upon which they can
> obtain forgiveness, would beg of their brethren to shed
> their blood, that the smoke might ascend to God as an
> offering to appease the wrath that is kindled against
> them, and that the law might have its course." Mormon
> *Journal of Discourses* 4:43.

She was a murderer, just as surely as if she had held the
weapon now in Mark's hand. In early Mormon days,
leaders such as Brigham Young himself preached the
doctrine of blood atonement for apostates who had
committed grievous sins, as the woman sleeping before
Mark had done. They could only achieve salvation

through their own death—in fact they should welcome it so they could "have their blood spilt upon the ground, that the smoke thereof might ascend to heaven as an offering for their sins."

She had murdered the person he had created, the brilliant student, the caring future physician, the fun-loving friend and family member.

Mark didn't notice Herbie, the big Maine coon cat he had bought Lori for her birthday shortly after the couple were married. The animal, accustomed to playing with both, was nearby, ever ready for a romp.

Herbie had again curled up with Lori on the bed after coming out from the hiding place he'd found during the fight. Mark had ignored him.

As he'd sat playing Nintendo on the television screen after she had gone to bed sobbing, the anger began to boil. It welled within him as his deft hands manipulated the controller skillfully, mindlessly playing the games he had loved since childhood. Over and over in his head he wrestled with the agony she had caused. Worse, his mind was muddled, dulled from being discovered in his lies. For two days now he had wrestled with the idea of killing her, then turned away in horror at the thought.

So many times before he had been adept at turning the conversation to his liking, not only with his wife, but with others. He was as good at the game of lies as he was at playing the game on the screen. He had played both since childhood. In many ways, the game of deception was more fun, more challenging, because the stakes were real—and high. He hadn't lost in recent years.

His fingers flew, manipulating the keypad by rote.

She was formidable in anger. Her intellect more than compensated for her diminutive size. Like a much larger dog intimidated by a tiny Yorkie, more than once, he had found that he was no match for her when they quarreled. This business of being a god on his own planet only went so far when it came to domestic arguments. No, he didn't want to face her again in the morning, because he simply wouldn't have any answers then.

He had been found out. In the morning, she would talk not only to him, but more important, to her mother, to his parents, to his brothers, to his sister who lived nearby in the same apartment complex. She would talk to their friends and acquaintances at the ward at the end of their street, and to her friends at the brokerage in the Wells Fargo building downtown.

And then tongues would wag. If there was one thing that he knew about growing up in Utah, when something went amiss among the brethren, it didn't take long for the entire state to know it. If nothing else, goodly portions of them were cousins. Utah is a state of close relationships—and relations. It is also a state where a passel of them are out each night at their local ward house or Temple doing the Lord's work, fulfilling the obligations set forth by their faith. They would talk, and the talk would be about him.

He would be discussed over the morning cup, not of coffee, forbidden to practicing Mormons, but of Postum, a grain beverage that has been the morning "pick-me-up" for many Mormon families for more than a century.

Mark Hacking had erred. It was now cover-up time.

In Mark's mind, feverishly working, but dulled by anxiety, he knew what lay before him as surely as he knew what they would say when they learned of his non-existent exams, or the admission to medical school that he had created out of thin air, or a host of other lies created to bolster his manufactured persona.

Without thinking, he rose, walked into the spare bedroom, dropped the letter he was holding, and picked up a gun, a .22 rifle. He placed the tiny round in its chamber. It was so simple. With a quick shot he would not have to face her again in the morning.

Would they excommunicate him for killing Lori? He didn't know. If they did, would it be short-lived? The sanctions hadn't been so bad when he had been sent home from his mission in disgrace. While away from home, Mark had drunk alcohol and smoked cigarettes and had done all manner of things proper Mormon boys weren't supposed to do.

But unbeknownst to his friends and family, Mark had brought the bad habits home with him.

"It was almost a joke to him," Paul Soares later recalled. "After Mark returned home he told me and Debora (my first wife) it was because of the injury to his back. I never thought much of it, but I wondered, since he looked okay—but with back injuries, you never know. I had kind of gotten hints from my mom and Lori that there was more to it than a back injury. In the LDS culture, when someone is sent home from their mission it is something that isn't talked about much."

Paul finally asked his brother-in-law point black if

his back was better from the accident. "He turned to me and said, 'Well, that's not the real reason I came home from my mission.'

"I just said, 'I figured so,' and that was it. I didn't know then what had happened, and I didn't know the extent of what Lori knew, if she knew anything at all. But knowing what I know now, I don't think she knew very much 'cause she wouldn't have accepted that."

Could he perform a sincere repentance and again become a practicing Saint, perhaps even get married again? He had a life before him, and damned if he would let her destroy it. And who knows? He might even get away with it. The plan was quickly forming in his muddled mind, swelled by the anger of exposure.

Mark stood before her, anger welling inside of him. Yet it was anger tinged with love. When she awoke, Lori would still know he had lied to her again, this time telling the whopper of all whoppers. Her knowledge of the lie wouldn't go away. And Lori had as much as told him in the letter that she was through covering up for him.

His decision was made.

Irrevocable.

A .22-caliber slug makes a tiny entry wound in the human head: it pierces the scalp, then crashes through the relatively thin quarter-inch–thick bone of the skull. It then tears through the meninges, the outermost covering of the brain, boring into the cerebral cortex, finally lodging at the point of most resistance, or exiting the head, flattened and tearing open a much larger exit wound of flesh, blood, and weeping brain tissue.

Killing is an art, he was learning. There would be a

sound of metal against metal as he cocked the .22-caliber killing machine. He only needed to avoid Lori waking. He walked ever so carefully into the other room, slid the round into the chamber, then slowly moved the firing pin into place behind the round.

Mark thought about it, his hand tightening on the gun. He couldn't allow her to feel the pain, the humiliation of facing others when his lie was exposed, as it surely would be. Mark determined that he must kill Lori for two reasons. First for challenging him and killing the persona he had created. But equally important, he must kill her to spare the tiny woman he adored the pain she would surely endure when he was found out.

Mark Hacking fired one shot directly into the head of his sleeping wife. She died instantly. The bald and bearded 6'2" hulk of a man stood over her, master of his home once again.

Mark went into the other room and sat down. After a while, he wondered if he had actually done what he thought he had. He returned to the bedroom and looked down at Lori lying there, dead, her head weeping blood.

Only Herbie remained, but he was nowhere to be seen now, retreating into his special hiding place in the couple's closet.

Yet Herbie, a predator, knew the smell of blood. His keen cat's senses told him that something unusual had happened in his habitat. He retreated even farther into the closet until he found the hole at the back. When Herbie retreated into his den, Mark and Lori sometimes didn't see him for days.

Now Lori needed to be disposed of. It would be like taking out the garbage. He would just put the body in a bag and take it to the Dumpster and let the City of Salt Lake Streets and Sanitation Division trucks take care of the rest, hauling it to the city dump.

And they would discard another piece of refuse, baggage unloved and unwanted. The garbage trucks would haul away his yet unborn child.

Mark Hacking watched his wife as she lay dead in the Mormon garments she would have no further need of wearing.

Chapter Two

The sun smiles upon Utah. It is the most geographically diverse state of any save Texas and Alaska. Landlocked, it even boasts a salt sea. In the northeast, the High Uintas soar to heights that close them for almost half the year. In the south, the Escalante Mountains do the same. The Wasatch, near Salt Lake City, covered in cedar, juniper, and aspen, offer a lush greenness at certain times of year that would rival the most verdant Louisiana swamp in color. The south's red rock canyons are filled with soaring sculptures touched by the hand of God and nature. It was in this blessed Eden that Mark Hacking and Lori Soares grew up.

They call it Zion.

In Utah, the name is everywhere. It is on banks, storefronts, churches, and schools. It is the state's word of choice to describe itself, even towering over the word Joseph Smith coined meaning *honeybee*, "Deseret." The state's symbol is the beehive. In fact, its highway signs boast the image of a hive that looks more like a capitol dome than anything else. Residents, true to their pioneer heritage, pride themselves on being as busy as bees in their industriousness.

The name of Zion also graces one of the nation's treasures and aptly describes it. Zion National Park, south of Cedar City, rivals other more famous parks to the north and west in its beauty and grandeur. The Virgin River flows south from there, cutting a deep canyon in Arizona before it arrives at Mesquite, Nevada, a stone's throw away from the Utah border. There, casino parking lots are jammed with the cars of the sin-starved citizens of the Beehive State.

The Church is everywhere, a fact of life as sure as death, taxes, and the need of life-giving water in a region that is mostly desert.

Mormonism is a religion of miracles and revelations. At the top of its hierarchy is the president and prophet, a mortal who has, through a very long life in the Church, inherited the mantle of a near papacy. Mormon presidents inherit the powers of prophecy upon their investiture. Like the Roman Curia, there are no women included in the hierarchy.

Mormons believe that their prophet speaks directly with God—and God speaks back.

The president and his two counselors even have an inner sanctum in the Salt Lake Temple in which they retire and pray for revelations. Such was the case just before the turn of the last century when the prophet had a revelation with far-reaching secular consequences.

In Utah the Church and its members are often known by the acronym L.D.S., for Latter-day Saints. The actual full name of the Church is The Church of Jesus Christ of Latter-day Saints.

News of the L.D.S. church is big news in the state's

press. Why? Because the denomination dominates every aspect of Utah life.

And the church control of media isn't confined to print. KSL, Salt Lake City's NBC affiliate is Church owned as well.

No law introduced in the stately capitol building on a hill overlooking Temple Square and the site of the founding of Salt Lake City gets past the watchful eye of the church. And precious few acts are passed into law without the endorsement of clerics in L.D.S. headquarters near Temple Square.

And Utah is clean, squeaky clean. It tolerates the sale of liquor in state-owned liquor stores. It sells mixed drinks in "private" clubs, a remnant of the temperance movement long ago abandoned in other states. For a hefty price, restaurants can secure a cocktail, beer, and wine license.

Devout Mormons such as Lori Hacking don't drink, smoke, or gamble. They are, however, a practical people who acknowledge and accept the foibles of unbaptized "Gentiles" as they call the rest of mankind. The Gentiles, in turn, joke about the straight-laced atmosphere in which the Mormons live. The tradeoff for them is an environment of good schools, low crime, and breathtaking beauty.

The Mormon prohibition against alcohol is ironic because much of the sect's history is replete with stories of the early Mormons' love of the grape. Joseph Smith, in fact, even operated a bar in a hotel owned by his family. His wife, however, quickly forced him to close it.

Clean living in Zion is serious business, and seemingly good for business as well.

There are even stores such as an Orem mom and pop video rental that boast, "Clean family-oriented movie store."

In early 2005, the Provo public library banned *The Weekly*, a respected alternative newspaper, saying there was no interest in the publication, despite the fact that it was picked up by 100 patrons per week. The librarian said that he had heard complaints about the *Weekly*'s provocative covers.

There are other throwbacks to a simpler time even in the state's largest city, on its most prominent street, State Street. The Wagon Wheel Square Dance Shop is devoted to costumes worn by square dancers harkening back the 1950s when the popular country dance fad was in its heyday.

State Street, 120 feet wide from the steps of the Capitol Building, runs straight as a buggy whip and bisects the city until it leaves town and turns into U.S. Hwy. 89. It then bisects the state, paralleling I-15, the Wasatch Mountains on one side, and the Great Basin on the other. It is said that Brigham Young, a master urban planner, designed the street and others like it in Salt Lake City, making them exceptionally wide so that a team of oxen pulling a prairie schooner could make a U-turn effortlessly. Other Utah towns boast broad avenues as well.

Most of the streets in Salt Lake City are numbered in a system virtually incomprehensible to newcomers until it is explained to them. The Fortieth Ward, a Mormon church near Mark and Lori Hacking's apartment building, has the address 630 East 100 South. Natives shorten the address to 630 E. 1st street south. All of the numbered streets in the city radiate from Temple Square, and their northerly, southerly, easterly, or westerly designation signifies their location in relation to the great Mormon Temple with its golden sculpture of the Angel Moroni almost touching the skies.

Nineteen-fifties and -sixties architecture stands untouched by urban renewal or a desire for more decorative and less ugly buildings. One-story motels dot the city's main thoroughfares, their owners prospering as they always have, untouched by chains of inns so common to other cities.

Salt Lake City, and much of the rest of Utah, experienced an ecclesiastical building boom in the two decades following World War II. Ward houses, the equivalent of a Gentile Christian church building, were built in cookie-cutter uniformity across the city and state, universally boring, but practical in their design, the church preferring to pour vast sums into its stately temples and vast business empire.

The ward houses, both large and small, are scattered across Utah by the thousands, one for every neighborhood. In Salt Lake City, their listing in the phone book occupies seven pages. They are as numerous as Catholic churches are surrounding the Holy See in Rome.

Stake Houses serve several Ward Houses. The Ward is the place where congregations of Mormons meet regularly, while the Stake Houses are for holding conferences several times a year.

Utah is by far the most conservative state in the Union, more so than the most traditional of the Deep

South. It is whiter as well. Black faces are rare, and
brown ones are more likely to belong to Native Americans than Mexican Americans. While Mexican restaurants have made their way into the state's towns and
cities, it isn't uncommon to find a restaurant serving eth-
nic food of a home-grown variety such as the Navajo
Hogan in Salt Lake City which boasts a Navajo taco, a
staple of Indian food served on "fry bread."

It is in this environment that Mark Hacking and Lori
Soares grew up.

The couple had met when Lori was a sophomore at
Orem High School. Mark was a year ahead of her. The
two were on a camping trip to Lake Powell. She had
made the trip with friends, a high school kid on an adventure in the wilderness.

Mormon kids from Orem are no different from
other teenagers across the nation. They are rowdy, rambunctious, adventuresome, and foolhardy. They believe
themselves to be indestructible and are careless when
prudence would be the more reasoned course to take.

She had paid little attention to the chunky red-
headed kid until he stuck his hands in the campfire to
turn over a log and got himself burned.

Lori, even at the age of 15, was a take-charge kind
of girl. She administered rudimentary first aid to him.
After a while, she asked his name.

"Mark, Mark Hacking," he replied. "Thanks for
helping me."

The conversation was an opening and Lori continued to sit with him, talking as the sting of the burn

intensified. She didn't know why she was sitting there, especially as the night grew long and others climbed into their sleeping bags. Toward daybreak, both dozed, fatigue getting the better of them.

The next day she called her mom, Thelma, back in Orem.

"I met a boy," she said, her hazel eyes glinting. "His name is Mark."

Thelma Soares and her daughter were best friends. Each found in the other a refuge. Often, it was the two of them against the world because of Thelma's divorce when Lori was in the fifth grade.

She had started life on New Year's Eve, 1976, in California, where Thelma and Eraldo Soares adopted her from LDS Social Services four months later. Earlier, they had adopted their son Paul from Los Angeles County Social Services at the age of three months.

The two had done their mission work together in Brazil, Eraldo's native country. Thelma learned to speak fluent Portuguese, and the two continued to speak the language at home throughout their marriage, teaching it to their children. Paul speaks fluent Portuguese today.

Paul remembers going to get Lori and bringing his new little sister home.

"We arrived at the adoption agency and while they were signing the papers, I thought it was like sitting with a finance manager buying a new car. I wandered off, and eventually found Lori. I ran in yelling, 'I found the baby!' "

The proud new parents brought her home in a tiny pink dress and a white lace bonnet, holding a pink-and-white stuffed rabbit. At three months, she found comfort, as most infants do, in a pacifier.

Paul admits being jealous of the newcomer at home. "I terrorized her to death, and I teased her," he remembers.

Parents save things, even the most trivial everyday items. One such item was a church receipt showing Lori's tithe, a penny for each year of her life. The Mormon Church wasn't getting rich off the child, but it was the thought that counted, and she was forming a habit that would last a lifetime. All good Saints are expected to give a ten percent tithe to the Church.

Thelma and Eraldo were living in Fullerton and when Lori grew older she started school at Pacific Drive Elementary. She was popular, outgoing, and smart.

But when the two parents split up in December 1987, mother and daughter moved to Utah to be among like-minded Mormons. The split from his daughter crushed Eraldo.

Paul stayed behind with his father in California. He lives there today near Disneyland. It was easier for a boy in his late teens, and soon going on a mission, to stay with his dad. For a fifth-grade girl, the upheaval was traumatic. Lori's bond with Thelma naturally grew as the two settled in at Orem.

In Orem, Lori was enrolled in Windsor Elementary School, and then later went to Orem's Canyon View Junior High.

Lori Soares began to shine, a bright star among the adolescents of the small town. She was smart, smarter than most, and she knew how to use her intelligence and popularity. By ninth grade, she was elected class president.

Orem was a great place for Lori to grow up. The snow-capped mountains tower over the town, giving the region the name Mountainland. It offers some of the nation's great outdoor recreation areas. While other areas of the country suffer through winter, the people of Orem revel in it. Here children learn to ski as easily and early as they learn hopscotch. Just up Provo Canyon, actor Robert Redford put a hamlet named Sundance on the map with a world-famous film festival. It had begun as a one-lift ski resort in the 1940s.

Growing up in Orem, Lori was surrounded by national parks, national forests, and national monuments. Here, in this fairy-tale region, waterfalls spew forth from the side of mountains and drop 500 feet. In the fall, the Aspen trees turn a bright gold before the area becomes a winter wonderland of ice and snow. Yet winter is gentle, a time for play, unlike that of the East, Midwest, and South. In Utah, the cold is comfortable, something to be respected, but not feared or hated.

Orem was a great place to grow up, and Lori Soares did so with gusto. She developed into a pretty girl with a chiseled face and sharp features highlighted by her bright eyes. She played on baseball teams and went to school dances. Meeting Mark was a highlight of her mounting interest in boys.

Lori spent hours with her two pals Holly and Rebecca Carroll as the three girls lounged around her bedroom talking—mostly about boys.

When she was 16, Eraldo had given Lori a blue Volkswagen bug, which became a badge of status and trust as she drove the broad streets of Orem with her two friends.

Lori was eager for independence, and as a single parent, Thelma welcomed it when her daughter found a job at the Orem Car Wash. The job wasn't prestigious, and being a wash girl was hard work but very quickly, Lori learned respect for money and what it could do for her.

Lori settled into high school with ease. Classes at Orem High were full, but not packed, with an average of about twenty in each, and the students were generally well off.

The school was 88 percent white, with a smattering of Blacks, Indians, Asians, and a few Hispanics. In standard testing, the students placed above average. Lori would receive a quality education during her high school years.

Into this safe and antiseptic world a popular, accident-prone kid moved as well. Unlike Lori, he had been born to a large Mormon family, prosperous and loved by the community. Mark Hacking, a red-headed guy with a face as open as a fried egg, and a smile as wide and welcoming as a Baptist revival, was popular in school. His look was worthy of central casting, the all-American kid complete with freckles and curly hair. He had a personality to match, having grown up with six brothers and sisters.

Such families provoke mirth, and even a little derision by non-Mormons as they drive down the street in any Utah town. No matter what make or model of car, van or SUV they are driving, Gentiles dub the car a BMW. The acronym stands for Big Mormon Wagon.

Mormons are encouraged by their faith to breed and populate the world. From its earliest days, church leaders encouraged the faithful to have families as large as the head of the household could support comfortably. Though many aspects of the practice of making babies for the faith—such as polygamy—have gone by the wayside due to outside social pressures, Mormon broods still tend to be large, and the family of Mark Hacking certainly fit the mold.

Dr. Doug Hacking practiced at the Cherry Tree office of Utah Pediatrics in Orem. Kids from all over Orem knew and loved him. He was kind and safe, the sort of doc who went out of his way for his patients and their families.

He was a product of Utah. He had attended undergraduate school at Brigham Young University in nearby Provo as the tumultuous 1960s faded. After his graduation, Doug went on to medical school in Wisconsin, followed by a residency at Columbus Children's Hospital.

The family moved into a house just off Center Street, in Orem. There Mark Hacking grew up with his brothers Lance, Scott, and Chad, and his sisters Tiffany, Sarah, and Julie. A skinny kid at first, he grew chunkier as he got older.

He was accident-prone, ever accident-prone, as his pal from childhood, Brandon Wood, remembered.

To Mormon families, the ward house is a second home. Often they spend six hours or more there on Sundays, not to mention the countless hours spent at church during the week. It was at one of these meetings that tiny Mark Hacking made one of his first speeches. Too small to reach the microphone, the curly-headed kid stood on a step stool to make himself heard. When he finished speaking, he forgot that he was standing on a stool and tumbled off the dais. Wood remembers that Mark came up smiling.

Brandon and Mark were good pals all through school. They went through Boy Scouts, played football, and did all of the boy things that would be expected. They had the mountains, the glorious Wasatch, as their playground where they could hike and climb to their hearts' content. For a boy growing up, Orem is as near paradise as it gets.

Hiking in the mountains above Orem is fabulous. Even trails near town offer spectacular views and secluded spots. It was below one of these, the Bonneville Shoreline Trail, which winds through the hills just above the town's cemetery that would someday be made briefly notorious by Mark Hacking as the burial spot of his wife.

Mark and his friends grew up on these trails, running, playing, sometimes getting lost, all of the things that young boys do outdoors, yet doing them in a place more scenic, more blessed, and simply more special than just about anyplace else in the country. And like children everywhere, many didn't appreciate what they had, because it was just, well, home.

For Mark, sports and the outdoors were all right, but they weren't the defining thing in his life. Mark Hacking genuinely liked people, and wanted them to like him. It was the most important thing in the world to him, an obsession. While Janet Hacking was doing the mom thing with her daughters—dance class and the like—Mark was making people around him laugh. He became the class clown.

Part of that was from his natural proclivity toward accidents. Mark could get himself into the damnedest messes, his friends remember. He didn't do it on purpose—he was just a klutz.

He could spin a yarn as good as the next guy, and often better. He was quick, with an agile mind that was able to grasp the humor of even the smallest things, the turn of a phrase, or a movement, a wisp of smoke or a rustling paper.

He was smart, as might be expected of the son of Orem's beloved pediatrician. Mark aspired to be an Eagle Scout, and any boy who has been through Scouting knows that to achieve the rank is an arduous task that only the very best, smartest, most skillful and talented Scouts get anywhere near doing. To be an Eagle Scout often presages success and greatness in later life. As often as not, though, it can be the high point of life achieved at much too young an age. Mark Hacking nearly peaked too soon—but in fact, didn't peak at all, because he didn't measure up. He didn't complete the required work to achieve the coveted rank.

Some of Mark's klutziness wasn't his fault. A fact of life in large families is hand-me-down clothes. Acquaintances remember how his shoes would sometimes come off when he kicked a ball. In fact, the shoes had been passed down from a brother who had outgrown them. Mark didn't mind though. It made people laugh and brought him the attention that he increasingly craved, the nourishment of his soul.

Friends remember an incident on a Scouting trip that was a definite attempt at getting attention, in a humorous sort of way.

He had slept near the fire, and had rolled into ashes, getting soot on his face. His fellow Scouts laughed at the dirty-faced boy. The next night, Mark slept elevated on a wooden platform that the children had erected. But the class clown wasn't above going the extra mile for a laugh, and before he went to bed he took a handful of ashes with him. The following morning he smeared them on his face before rising. The other scouts were amazed that he still had awakened with soot on his face, despite the fact that he was elevated and away from the fire.

It is the earliest example of Mark Hacking going to elaborate means to contrive a deception, and it took planning. Brandon Wood would later remember the incident.

"We couldn't figure it out," he recalled. "Weird, goofy stuff happened to him."

Mark Hacking had begun honing his skills as a master of deceit.

Just as comedians and actors sharpen their acts, and athletes spend years polishing and improving their natural abilities, Mark Hacking now worked toward his goal, either consciously or unconsciously. In the shadow of his overachieving father and brothers, Mark found that it was easier to get through life by creating a world of his own, a façade for the rest of the world to see. It started small, but it started, and there was no turning back. At the age of 12, Mark Hacking was exhibiting clear manifestations of the personality disorder that would ultimately lead to his destruction, and in the end, cost the girl who had fallen in love with him her life.

Chapter Three

People are not born liars. The art of fabrication isn't a congenital trait. It is a learned one.

Mark Hacking learned it well, practiced it, and honed the skill from boyhood. The problem was that nobody in his busy and extremely successful family took the time to recognize his problem. His pediatrician father should have noticed that something was out of place with his son. His brother, who himself would become a doctor, should have as well. There is an element of psychiatry that every would-be doctor encounters in medical school.

Narcissistic personality disorder, and its attendant problem of habitual lying from early adolescence on to inflate an otherwise poor self-image, are well documented in psychiatric texts. More than half of those who suffer from it are males. The estimates of prevalence of the disorder vary wildly, from 2 to 16 percent in the clinical population and less than 1 percent in the population as a whole.

Psychiatrists and psychologists use nine criteria to diagnose an individual suffering from narcissism. Five or more of them must be met to classify a person as a narcissist.

> Feels grandiose and self important (exaggerates accomplishments, talents, skills, contacts, and personality traits to the point of lying, and demands to be recognized as superior without commensurate achievements.);

> Is obsessed with fantasies of unlimited success, fame, fearsome power or omnipotence, unequaled brilliance (the cerebral narcissist), bodily beauty or sexual performance (the somatic narcissist), or ideal, everlasting, all-conquering love or passion;

> Is firmly convinced that he or she is unique and, being special, can only be understood by, and should only be treated by, or associate with, other special, unique, or high-status people or institutions;

> Requires excessive admiration, adulation, attention and affirmation—or, failing that, wishes to be feared and notorious;

> Feels entitled. Demands an automatic and full compliance with unreasonable expectations for favorable treatment;

> Is "interpersonally exploitative," i.e., uses others to achieve his or her own ends;

> Is devoid of empathy. Is unable or unwilling to identify with, acknowledge, or accept the feelings, needs, preferences, priorities, and choices of others;

> Is constantly envious of others and seeks to hurt or destroy the objects of his frustration. Suffers from persecutory (paranoid) delusions as he believes that

others feel the same about him or her and are likely to act similarly;

Behaves arrogantly and haughtily. Feels superior, omnipotent, omniscient, invincible, immune, "above the law," and omnipresent (magical thinking). Rages when frustrated, contradicted, or confronted by people he considers inferior to and unworthy of him.*

Of the nine criteria needed to diagnose the disorder, Mark Hacking clearly met six of them. His lying was well developed when he joined one of the largest sales forces on earth, the 60,000-strong army of Mormon missionaries who are fanned out around the globe on a daily basis. He had become a glib talker, adroit at promoting the ideas his fertile mind had concocted. His missionary training would only enhance the ability to convince the doubters he encountered. In Mark, a young elder leaving the safe haven of Orem, the Church could not have asked for a more outwardly confident representative to hawk the faith to the Gentiles of his mission.

He would serve two years, from the age of 19, at his parents' complete expense. Mark would be one of 40 percent of young Mormon men who voluntarily do missionary work for the Church. Ninety-three percent of Mormon missionaries are of college age, many taking a leave of absence from undergraduate studies. Women are also allowed to serve on missions. They have the title of "sister," and don't begin their service until they are age 21. They serve for eighteen months.

*The criteria are taken and condensed from *Diagnostic and Statistical Manual of Mental Disorders* fourth edition, text revision (DSM IV-TR). The American Psychiatric Association (2000).

Some missionaries pay their own way, while those in less fortunate circumstances have their expenses paid by their congregations.

Becoming a missionary is not automatic. Prospects are interviewed to determine if they are worthy of going out into the world to represent the Church to the Gentiles. In fact, it is said that the biggest test of the missionaries is to not become disheartened in the face of rejection, having doors slammed in their faces, or being told day after day that they are talking nonsense. It is perhaps an underlying reason that so many Mormons go into sales as their life's work, and why Utah is the state with the largest number of multi-level marketing businesses in the world.

Yet sometimes missionaries get into trouble.

Mark Hacking would have his own problems meeting the rigid standards of being a Mormon missionary. Early on he joined legions of the Church's fallen angels and tarnished saints.

Mark began his missionary work as most Mormon boys do, happy to enjoy a rite of passage as normal and natural as puberty. Like millions before him, he would rise at 6:30 a.m., eat a hearty breakfast, and put on a snow-white shirt over the sacred garments that true believers know will protect them from harm. He would then don a tie, and finish the uniform with a pair of shiny shoes.

Mormon missionaries are not permitted to discuss some of the more "different" tenets of the faith's theology. Moreover, many, if not most, of the ceremonies performed in the Temple are secret, forbidden by sacred oath (until recently, on pain of death) from being discussed with those who are not "Temple worthy."

Prospective missionaries fill out a simple form and send it to the Salt Lake City headquarters of the Church. Rudimentary questions are asked, but there is also an emphasis on foreign language skills because the Mormon Church's proselytizing is increasingly going beyond U.S. shores. A couple of months later, after General Authorities of the Church pray over placement, the destination of each missionary is chosen.

In fact, missionaries are taught that their "call" is divine in nature. They will go to do their mission work in the place God wants them to go. Their toil, and sometimes suffering and on rare occasions even death, is the will of God. Should they die, not to worry. In Mormon theology, there is no such place as Hell.

After being chosen, Missionaries are treated to their first Temple ceremonies, where they learn over a three-hour period the secrets that they are sworn not to reveal to the converts they are trying to recruit.

They are also introduced to Temple garments, which they are almost never to remove, the exceptions being for swimming, showering, and vigorous sports such as jogging.

Mark, like thousands before him, emerged from the Temple an elder not quite ready to face the world. He was lucky because the Missionary Training Center near the campus of BYU is just a few miles from Orem. It was there that he joined other Mormon youths for total immersion training in proselytizing for the faith. He entered a strange world of focus, where there were no books except scriptures, no music save hymns, no TV, movies, or even magazines. It was the tried-and-true LDS method of charging up its brigades.

After graduation, the missionaries took leave of their families, were handed a plane ticket, and sent off into the world with two suitcases and a backpack, and nothing more.

The mission is many Mormon youths' first experience with the unfamiliar. The city, town, or country to which they are dispatched is uncharted territory. Their housing is strange, without the comforts of home. Most importantly, their companion, the fellow missionary with whom their lives will become entwined 24/7, is a total stranger, and before the mission is over, there may be as many as fifteen different partners. They are never to be out of view, or earshot, of their fellow missionary.

They can't do anything alone, and if a bodily function calls, the missionary is supposed to wait nearby until their friend emerges from the bathroom.

Mormon missionaries are not slackers; Mark Hacking was to learn that the hard way. There is no room for the frivolity of play. After arising, he, like all of his cohorts, was required to spend an hour or two studying scripture, and then playing "investigator," a sort of role-play between a potential convert and a missionary. By 10 a.m., the missionaries hit the streets, whether in New York City or Moscow.

They pass out brochures on street corners. They knock on doors, they witness, attempting to pass on a message from Jesus Christ. It is hard work and most often thankless. Frequently they are met with ridicule.

But sometimes there is success as well. Sometimes the investigator, as the potential convert is called, actually converts. The Mormon missionaries are very, very good at what they do.

Elder Mark Hacking was the district leader. He certainly looked the part, with his clean-cut open face and abundant wavy red hair. Mark and his pal Brandon Wood even posed for a photo sporting white shirts, ties, and dark pants, the trademark Mormon missionary look familiar to many Americans.

Mark drew a good card for his mission and didn't suffer any such discomfort. He would do his work for the Church in Winnipeg, Manitoba. The town couldn't have been more of a contrast to Orem.

It is as flat as a toad squashed on a Utah freeway.

Salt Lake City and Orem kiss the heavens at about a mile in elevation. Much of the Canadian province where he was dispatched to for his mission hovers at between 600 to 900 feet, with flatland as far as the eye can see.

But Winnipeg isn't a bad town, despite its lack of soaring vistas or the elegance of a Wasatch landscape. A college town, with all of the trappings and temptations that come with it, it boasts both the University of Manitoba, and the University of Winnipeg. It even has a professional football team, the Winnipeg Blue Bombers of the Canadian Football League.

And it was here that an accident-prone Utah kid who craved being the center of attention first spread his wings, using the excuse of a Mormon mission to live more freely than he ever had before—free from the strict confines of life in Utah where everyone watches everyone else, where everyone makes it their business to know their neighbor's business, and if someone gets out of line or strays from the righteous path of orthodoxy, to report it to the ward leaders.

Not all missionaries remained Mormon after a taste of the other side. A fellow missionary got into deep trouble when a girl he was dating became pregnant. He was quickly sent packing so as not to contaminate the purity of his fellow Mormon youths. Another elder, Travis Webb, said that despite the fact that Mark and Lori had dated throughout high school, he never heard Mark mention her during their mission days.

Mark began seeing girls, staying alone with them in their apartments, and watching movies, a serious violation of the missionary's rules.

Mark had been popular with the Orem High School Golden Tigers class of '94. To them, he was just a normal guy, as his close friend Brandon Wood remembered. He had his faults, but "we all do."

"I don't want to paint him as an angel, he's not an angel," his friend says. "Mark has always been a great person. He always had a very big heart."

His faults began to overwhelm his better side. It was on the mission that Mark became a smoker, in direct contravention of the Word of Wisdom that he was supposed to live by for health purposes. With his outgoing character, he also became a bit of a party animal.

It isn't unusual for missionaries to not measure up to the strict standards that are expected of them. The schedule is demanding, with the workday ending at 10:30 p.m. The thought of nightlife is hopeless, and because Mormons who strictly follow Joseph Smith's Word of Wisdom are forbidden drugs, drink, tobacco, coffee, R-rated flicks, masturbation, or any activity beyond kissing with the opposite sex, pastimes used for relaxation by a large number of American youth are denied to them. In a way, the religion exacts a cruel toll on those asked to spread its joy to the uninitiated. As they are thrust into the real world on their own for the first time, they are denied some of life's sweetest pleasures. They must withdraw from that world. The missionaries can't read books and listen to music unless they are from the church, and they force themselves into denial of the things that they grew up with, such as movies, television and even a daily newspaper.

Thursdays are for writing home, but a phone call is prohibited, except on the Hallmark Holiday of Mother's Day, and the Christian holiday, Christmas.

Many get homesick. Others find love. It isn't uncommon for young female investigators to fall in love with the clean-cut young men who are trying to convert them. Men being men, sometimes the sins of the flesh get the better of what they were taught back in missionary school.

Today's male missionaries have it better than their elders did in one respect. They no longer are required to wear the full suit in inclement climates such as Houston, where old-time missionaries during summer months earned a special place in Mormon paradise for enduring the discomfort of three layers of clothing on their upper bodies.

For Mormon parents, the failure of a child in his mission is an embarrassment, an admission of inadequacy in their child-rearing, and a disgrace that is public for all in the tightly knit community to see.

Webb was stunned when his district leader was sent

packing from Winnipeg for an unceremonious return to Salt Lake City.

"I was very surprised when he ended up being sent home, and when I found out later [what had happened], that is what blew me away," he recalled ten years later to a reporter with the *Deseret Morning News*.

"I think he got a taste of freedom and did a little bit of lying with the girlfriend up there, and maybe came home and had the pressure of going back and getting into regular life," he said.

In retrospect, Webb was certain that Mark had created a suitable cover story for anybody who asked why he had returned to Zion.

"I think he had to make up some lies to tell his family as to why he came home early, and lying became easier and easier for him because he was getting out of things."

Mark still retained his ability to spin a yarn that sounded completely believable to others. When he returned to Orem, family, and friends, he was the same solicitous, courteous, young man he had appeared to be since childhood.

He was fun to be around, outgoing, entertaining, and still that big red-headed klutz with such endearing qualities.

Mark and Lori had dated off and on throughout high school. After Mark returned from his unsuccessful mission to Winnipeg, the relationship deepened.

Lori Soares checked into LaSalle dorm at Weber State University in 1995, a tiny kid with an olive complexion and a head of long, curly brown hair that fell below her shoulders. The campus, nestled in the hills of Ogden an hour north of Salt Lake, was far enough away from Orem for a spirited young girl to spread her wings, and as a state university, it was beyond the reach of the Church. By all accounts, Lori didn't go wild, and remained the fun-loving, studious kid she had been all through high school.

Her roommate, Heidi Gregory, describes her as "hilariously blunt" as well as "sarcastic and feisty."

Others knew her as a "spitfire." No matter what the description, Lori Soares was fun to be around.

After the year at Weber, Lori was ready for the big time, the beautiful modernistic campus of the University of Utah overlooking the Salt Lake Valley.

The campus is nestled into the Wasatch foothills. It looks across the valley toward the Oquirrh Mountains to the southwest, and the Great Salt Lake glimmering each day under the setting sun.

She found a home at the university in the business department, one of the nation's best. For a time, she saw the much bigger world of Washington when she served an internship with a firm in Chevy Chase. The sojourn was set up by the university's Hinckley Institute.

Her brother, Paul, visited her there, seeing her thrive in that rough-and-tumble world.

"I had such pride and joy in knowing she was my little sister," he said of the trip.

Back home in Utah, when she returned to the university, Lori and a group of girls took breaks from their studies as they danced in the dorm's halls with all of the high jinks and spontaneity of youth. In Lori's case, it was only to release the tension brought on by serious-minded study. She made the dean's list every semester that she was enrolled.

The girls had outings to the Olive Garden restaurant near campus, gorged themselves on ice cream, and then felt guilty about doing so, and also frequented Jake's Over the Top for shakes.

Lori's best friend, Heidi Gregory, was a live wire as well, always on the go, always ready for an adventure, a blond with a brunette, both cute as kittens and ready for whatever life was going to throw at them.

The two had a spirit of wanderlust. They wanted to see the country beyond Utah, the country that they'd seen on television and read about in books. They watched for cheap airline fares and took advantage of them, traveling to Savannah and Atlanta. Their greatest adventure was a trip on the red-eye to New York City for a riotous New Year's Eve in Times Square, two of Utah's best taking on the Big Apple just for fun. They didn't even rent a hotel room, Heidi remembers.

"She was the only person I met who could keep up with me," she said after Lori's death.

But Lori was a private person as well.

Just after the two became roommates, Heidi saw a photo of Lori and her mother.

"You don't look a bit like your mom," Heidi commented.

"I know," Lori replied without hinting that she had been adopted, characteristically sealing her innermost secrets away, a trait that would later prove fatal.

It wasn't just the new girlfriends and academics that occupied her time and thoughts. Mark was becoming an increasing presence in her life.

Yet there was a nagging feeling that she didn't tell anybody about, a troubling thing that made her question her relationship. She was aware that he had come home from his mission early, and that would bother any young Mormon girl intent upon a marriage sealed in the Temple.

Lori held the information about his return inside herself, not telling Heidi what she knew about it. If she even knew the truth, Mark Hacking's secret about how he was kicked off the mission died with her. Heidi knew, however, that it troubled Lori.

"She was bugged by it because she didn't think he'd given her a straight answer," she later told an interviewer. "I'm sure she dealt with it with him later, but I never knew about it."

Despite her misgivings, Mark and Lori grew closer every day and intense liking turned into intense love, and shortly before her graduation with honors from the University of Utah, the two were married in the soaring white Temple in Bountiful high above the Great Salt Lake.

She told her friends that the marriage was perfect and they were certain that she believed every word she told them. Her big klutz of a man was smart. She was certain that he was going to make something of himself—maybe be a doctor like his father. The couple would have babies and raise a family of their own in the Mormon tradition.

The couple was the pride of both Lori's parents.

While Thelma was nearby, Eraldo was a twelve-hour drive away in California. His visits were confined to trips to Utah when he came with his new wife and two new young children to see his daughter.

The family would check into a hotel for Christmas, set up a tiny tree in the room, and celebrate the Yuletide as best they could.

Chapter Four

"I have no wife whom I love so well that I would not put a javelin through her heart, and I would do it with clean hands . . ."

—Brigham Young, *Journal of Discourses*, vol. 3, p. 247

Mark Hacking looked down at the mass that was once his wife. He felt nothing but anger, no remorse, no sadness, nothing whatsoever other than the rage that had driven him to kill Lori. She lay still and quiet in their king-size bed, the place where, in all likelihood, the two had conceived the child that she had begun to tell friends that she was carrying.

Like almost all young women, the prospect of motherhood had fulfilled a dream for her.

Lori thought of raising a child that was her own flesh and blood with joyous expectation. Their child would not be adopted as she had been. It would know its real parents. Mark would be a wonderful father, despite his faults. He would teach their son or daughter—the first of many, she hoped—the way to live life having fun.

She'd yet to tell Thelma the news of her pregnancy, even in the email she'd sent on Thursday. Her mom had wanted her to attend a Friday night performance of the Mormon Tabernacle Choir. Lori declined, saying that she and Mark were already committed to go to a party that her co-workers at Wells Fargo were throwing for them.

Prospective fatherhood wasn't good news to Mark. The advent of a child complicated matters for him and the elaborate ruse he had dreamed up that was now so out of control.

Lori's head lay on the pillow still bleeding. How long would that last? Mark wondered.

Mark's mind was still dulled by rage, but in spite of that, he was at least aware that he had just committed murder, and that his problems now went far beyond being caught telling a lie by his wife. He had to dispose of her body. He would also have to account for her disappearance. There were so many details now, and the stakes were high for him, higher than they had ever been.

One thing at a time, deal with one thing at a time.

"I need a cigarette," he thought, almost smiling now that he would be able to smoke in the apartment.

Little more than an hour earlier, he and Lori had gone to the Maverik store for soft drinks. The two were spent from the fight, and Lori'd wanted something to drink before she went to bed.

The two had entered the double doors, Lori first,

wearing a gray T-shirt and baggy teal hospital scrubs, followed by Mark, dressed in Bermuda shorts and a T-shirt as well. Lori's luxuriant hair was pulled up into a high ponytail.

The store was quiet when they came in. Paul, the clerk behind the counter, had seen the couple before. The store was modern, clean, with a red-brick base on its exterior wall, and pink stucco up to a white cornice. MAVERIK, in bold red letters, hung from the center of the building.

Security cameras caught every transaction at the cash register and every movement throughout the store. It was hard to rob a Maverik store and not get your picture taken.

Paul paid little attention to the couple, only noticing that the husband, or boyfriend, of the attractive woman didn't buy smokes as he usually did.

While Lori was buying sodas, Mark asked the store clerk not to tell his wife that he was a smoker.

A timer on the store's videotape had clocked their entrance at 9:19 p.m., July 18, 2004.

The nicotine addiction again broke his attention span. His lungs ached for a smoke. Perhaps she would stop bleeding if he took a minute to go to the Maverik and buy cigarettes.

Mark walked to the bathroom that separated the two bedrooms of the apartment and washed his hands, subconsciously wanting to remove the kill from them. He looked at them to see if the murder had left any telltale signs.

Mark then took off the khaki shorts he had been

wearing and put on a pair of scrubs, the loose and comfortable cotton pants worn by operating room personnel worldwide. He put on a pair of flip-flops.

Mark Hacking walked out the door of Apartment #7. He got in Lori's gray Chrysler Sebring, adjusted the seat and mirror, turned around in the parking lot, and drove the few blocks to the clean pink store.

For the second time that night, Mark walked through the double doors of the Maverik and went up to the counter where the clerk was waiting to serve him. This time, he asked for a package of cigarettes. When the clerk turned his back to fetch them, Mark Hacking looked down, scratching the palm of his left hand with his right index finger.

He looked at the palms of both hands, searching for Lori's blood. He found none.

Mark left the store and tore open the pack when he reached Lori's car, quickly lighting up, and pulling the smoke deeply into his lungs, the nicotine instantly calming him. He hoped that the smoke would clear his head, because now he had important work to do, work that would afford him no mistakes.

He had to complete his task before morning, minimizing the risk of detection. He tossed the butt of the cigarette out the window and pulled the Chrysler back into the apartment parking lot, looking around for witnesses.

Mark backed the car up to the apartment's patio gate, which opened to the parking lot.

He re-entered the apartment and picked up a large hunting knife, and walked back into the bedroom.

She lay on the bed as he had left her, still, dead. The blood no longer seeped from her head, but it had saturated the pillowtop mattress that she lay upon.

Mark took the knife and penetrated the fabric of the pillowtop. It was tough, more like canvas than he had expected. He began to cut it, separating it from the rest of the mattress, removing it so that he could dispose of the bloody evidence.

But he had to get Lori off the thing. Her dead weight made her feel much heavier than she was when she had jumped up into his arms over the years.

Mark returned to the kitchen and got some large garbage bags and placed his wife in them so that blood would not drip on the carpet, or the sidewalk, or the parking lot asphalt. Like the pillowtop, Lori was now nothing more than garbage to him, evidence that must be disposed of if he was going to continue to have a reasonable life, on his terms, in the future.

The light red-brick walls of 127 South Lincoln were subdued in the early morning darkness, its six natural wood balconies silhouettes against the darker gray trim of each front apartment.

The building was a testament to entrepreneurship, built as a small project to bring in a modest but respectable income to its owner. The location is ideal. Situated near enough to downtown it would afford clerical workers nice housing; close enough to the state capitol building and other state offices to provide a home to Utah's lower level bureaucrats; close enough to LDS church headquarters to provide shelter to the workers who serve the vast network of Mormon wards, stakes, and enterprises; and importantly close enough to the university that it would provide upscale student housing.

Now it was a murder scene. The only thing missing was yellow-and-black crime-scene tape. That would come soon enough.

If Lori's body was found, Mark determined, it simply wouldn't do for her to be wearing Mormon garments. He quickly removed them and re-dressed her in jogging clothes.

Mark wrapped the body in garbage bags and the bloody pillowtop he had cut from the mattress. He picked up Lori's limp body, careful not to trip on the boxes that they'd left everywhere around the bedroom in preparation for the move to North Carolina.

He carried the body out of the bedroom, careful not to knock over the TV set next to the door leading to the living room. He took her through the patio doors, and struggled to place the awkward form into the back seat of his SUV.

He retrieved the gun and brought it to the car as well, then returned to the apartment.

There was one more trip. He removed the mattress from the apartment and carried it to the car for disposal.

The mattress was not heavy for a man the size of Mark Hacking, but it was unwieldy. He had to be quiet as he removed it to the car, careful not to bang the walls. Finally, he tugged and pulled the thing on top of his SUV, balancing it for a short ride to the nearest Dumpster.

Mark Hacking had accomplished his first mission without a flaw. He had removed his wife, as well as most of the evidence, from the murder scene.

Once he was free of Lori he could create any persona he liked, be anybody he wanted to be, with no interference from a prying spouse.

Mark inserted the key into the ignition, put the car into reverse, then into drive as he crept across the smooth asphalt surface of the lot.

He was careful not to go over a large drain grate situated right in the middle of the drive, fearful of risking a bump. He straddled it so as not to tip the precariously balanced mattress off the roof of the car.

Lincoln Street dead-ended into the Ward House. From the front, the building was deceptively small. In its rear, the church was more like a vast school, a warren of classrooms for Mormon meetings. Behind this maze of rooms was a Dumpster.

Mark eased the car across the deserted street and into the church parking lot.

There was so much to think about now, so very much.

Was Lori's head oozing blood again? If it got on the carpet of the car, he would have to rip that out and dispose of it. Could it soak through to the metal? Could he get the blood off that as well? He still felt that he hadn't removed all of it from his hands. It was with him now even as he carried the refuse to the dump.

There was so much to think about now, so very much.

Lori wouldn't show up at work tomorrow, and she was obsessive about getting to the Wells Fargo office, where she worked as an assistant broker, on time each morning. That was one of the things that annoyed him about his wife. She was so perfect, so damned perfect—unlike him.

As he drove, the fog lifting somewhat, he began to develop a plan in his mind.

Mark Hacking was now fully aware of what he had just done. He was fully aware that there were serious consequences to murder. He was confident in his ability to fabricate answers to what had happened, answers to her turning up missing.

Ahead, he saw the Dumpster. His first priority was to get rid of the bloody mattress. He knew that the longer he carried it, the more likely he would attract attention, maybe even the attention of the Salt Lake police.

He pulled up to the Dumpster and wrestled the mattress off the roof of the car, awkwardly manhandling it into the trash bin, then looked at his shirt, and yet again at his hands, satisfied that there was no blood on him. He was clean. Mark got back into the car. Half of his work was done, but the more important job lay ahead. Lori was still wrapped in garbage bags. He had to get rid of her and do it quickly before sunlight made everything more difficult.

Dawn would bring traffic, even recognition. Mark and Lori were popular in the university-based Ward where they were active. They were both popular at work, and neither had been shrinking violets growing up in Orem. They both had friends and relatives from childhood nearby. Mark's sister even lived in the same apartment complex.

Mark drove mindlessly, heading toward the campus that he knew so well. He passed the stadium, scene of so many Saturdays of glory for the Utes, the University of Utah football team. The giant coliseum had been the scene of other glories for the state as well. It was there that the colorful opening ceremonies of the Winter Olympics had been held while every Utahan's heart burst with pride. Things like that didn't happen every day in the City of Zion where the annual Pioneer Days festivities was as good as it got—excepting perhaps a win by the Utah Jazz at the Delta Center across downtown.

He continued his leisurely night drive along East 400 south toward the stadium, following the street as it jogged around Faultline Park before straightening out again to become East 500 South passing between Rice Eccles Stadium and Mount Olivet Cemetery, the last resting place of many of Salt Lake City's most illustrious citizens.

Mark drove aimlessly, mindlessly. He was on autopilot, heading toward the campus, and to the psychiatric hospital on its south side where he worked as an orderly. He remembered a Dumpster behind the hospital.

Mark's thoughts now turned briefly to suicide as a flash of what he had done to Lori brought him momentarily to his senses.

As he drove, he remembered long walks he'd taken with his sister Sarah. He had told her that he sometimes thought of killing himself, describing patients at the hospital who had taken their own lives. It was surely a relief to them to put their troubles behind them once and for all.

His mind returning to the business at hand, he thought of the Dumpster behind the hospital. Crews would come, maybe even at daybreak, to load the heavy receptacles and take the accumulated garbage away. He reflected on the men who drove the trash trucks. Their work was so common compared to his. He was the best that the University of Utah's Neuropsychiatric Unit had for what he did, which was mostly make patients laugh. Mark was popular at the hospital, and he knew it. Even if somebody did see him dumping something in the early morning hours, he had little fear that he would be questioned. He could just say that he had been cleaning and that the Dumpster at his apartment was overflowing, as it often did. As to the hour, Mark could tell anybody who asked that he just thought he would get an early start on his day. Plausible. Utah is a state where early risers are the norm, not the exception.

But there would be other questions that wouldn't be so easily handled, he knew. Questions would arise very quickly regarding Lori's absence. They would likely come first from her co-workers at Wells Fargo, but those would undoubtedly be followed in quick succession with questions from his family, and her mother and father.

Mark drove on as his mind worked feverishly to devise a plan.

The road rose imperceptibly as Mark neared the campus. A passenger would be unaware that he was climbing a hill if his eyes were closed, so gently does the grade rise as Salt Lake City's streets near the University of Utah campus. Mark was now driving with a goal in mind: the shipping dock and its Dumpster.

Below, the City of Zion sparkled, its lights creating magic in the darkness, hiding a somewhat drab mostly one-story town and transforming it into a carpet of light in the morning darkness. The view from campus is spectacular. Just up the mountain from the campus, Brigham Young had first laid eyes on the Salt Lake Valley and the river named Jordan that ran through it.

"This is the place," he told the pioneers who had faced unbearable hardship on the Mormon trail as it wound across the Midwest from Missouri.

The exodus of the Latter-day Saints is one of America's great adventures, and Mormons feel deservedly proud of what their ancestors had done as they escaped persecution after their leader and prophet was brutally murdered.

Mark Hacking wasn't thinking about Brigham Young and the Saints of yore as he drove toward the campus and the waiting Dumpster at the University of Utah's Neuropsychiatric Unit.

Mark knew that the spot would be deserted, and that it would be a good place to dump Lori's body.

He slowed as he reached his workplace and did a quick survey. As he expected, the front was deserted, and Mark was certain that the area around the loading dock would be as well. To his right, Salt Lake City shined below him, its lights rivaling the stars in the early morning darkness.

He turned left onto the street that ran its half moon–shaped course around the hospital. Immediately to his left, the loading dock emerged, and he slowly pulled the car up next to the Dumpster. There was no one to be seen.

He emerged from the car and picked up Lori's body. She was heavier than he would have expected as he lifted her high over the steel rim of the Dumpster and let go, quickly hearing a thud as she hit the surface of the garbage below.

Lori Soares was no longer a part of his life. The girl who had nursed his burnt hand at the age of 14 was now nothing more than organic waste to be deposited in a distant landfill. Mark had put her behind him. He was now ready to move on, without the danger that the life and persona he had created would be undone. He would go on to North Carolina after a suitable period of angst over his missing wife. What else could he do? What else would a reasonable world expect him to do?

A new life awaited him in the east—alone. Anybody would understand his wanting to get on with his life as a medical student in North Carolina. Anybody would understand why he would want to leave Salt Lake and its painful memories.

The whole thing seemed so plausible to him. If he could just get through the next few days, he was home free. In his mind, his moves thus far had been well thought out, well planned.

But Mark Hacking was an amateur at murder, and a rookie in the art of body disposal.

Universities, if nothing else, have deep pockets, and in the period since September 11, 2001, they, like other state agencies, have spared no expense on security. The Neuropsychiatric Institute was the subject of intense and constant surveillance by sixteen motion-sensitive closed-circuit television cameras beaming digital images into a central computer. The cameras captured the image of what appeared to be a man carrying a body wrapped in a cloth and tossing it into one of the Dumpsters provided to the university by Waste Management, the giant refuse company.

Yet the image was of poor quality. The video cameras installed by the campus were not designed to catch a killer disposing of evidence. Had the resolution been better, Mark Hacking's well-planned crime could have been undone with a solid identification of the perpetrator from the security video.

Chapter Five

Garbage trucks travel to the city dump at the rate of twelve per minute, sometimes more, sometimes less. Salt Lake City's dump is behind high levees hiding it from the rest of the world, save in one respect: It is on the flight path to Salt Lake's airport. For passengers approaching from the south, it is the last thing that they see before landing in the City of Saints.

Other birds fly over the dump as well. They are jokingly called Mormon Seagulls, lured from the Great Salt Lake like flying rats looking for a cheap meal.

A pink sign with raised green letters attests that the trucks are arriving at the Salt Lake Valley Solid Waste Facility. They lumber past the sign to check into the dump and deposit the contents. The vast landfill is one of 1,858 remaining in the United States, a number that has continually shrunk since 1988 when there were more than 8,000. Capacity in the nation's dumps has remained constant and new ones are much larger than landfills have historically been.

Dust hangs in the air, raised by the large trucks thundering by on California Street, a surprisingly well-paved divided highway that bisects a gently rolling prairie. To the north, beyond the airport lies the Great Salt Lake, a vast remnant of a salt sea that once covered the Great Basin during prehistoric times.

Officialdom transforms the word *garbage* into "Municipal Solid Waste," or MSW for short. Such is the nomenclature of government bureaucrats. The Salt Lake dump is the end destination of product packaging, grass clippings, furniture, clothing, bottles, food scraps, newspapers, appliances, paint, and batteries.

Organic materials such as yard trimmings account for slightly more than 12 percent of what ends up in our city dumps. Food scraps account for another 11 percent. It is the decomposition of this matter that produces the characteristic unpleasant odor of a landfill.

Gardeners are familiar with what makes the odor, the process that happens as organic matter decomposes and is turned into compost. So are cooks. The material creates a heat source without flame as the chemical components of organic matter give off energy. The energy slowly bakes the material much the same way that an oven bakes a solid piece of meat and turns it into a tender roast, the meat peeling off the bone with the touch of a fork.

Any organic matter deposited in the dump is quickly transformed into something far different from what it was just a few days before. The same goes for a human body.

Mark pulled away from the hospital, content that he hadn't been seen, confident that he could now move on to the next phase of creating his new life. He retraced the route he had driven, no longer fearful of seeing flashing police lights.

There was little time for him to come up with a story. The sun would soon rise, and Salt Lake City residents would go back to work after a summer weekend. One of those workers was expected to be Lori Hacking, an up-and-coming would-be stockbroker at Wells Fargo's office at Main and 3rd downtown.

A chill running up his spine, Mark began obsessing over the thought that he had blood on his hands or on the car. He was a typical guy, sometimes sloppy when it came to staying clean and keeping things clean. Old habits die hard, and no matter how many times he washed his hands, he knew that a chance remained he would miss something that would prove his undoing.

Had he missed something? Was the apartment a mess? Was there blood on the asphalt where he had carried Lori's body from the apartment to the car? He had to know.

Mark headed again toward the apartment on Lincoln where he now lived alone. He had to know if he needed to clean things up before someone came there, perhaps a friend, perhaps a family member, or God forbid, even the police.

Murder is hard work. It requires thought and concentration if it is to be successful. It also requires discipline.

Mark Hacking certainly had the discipline, as far as that went. He could conjure up a story with the best of them, and make it believable. But that was a different kind of discipline, and what's more, the challenge of doing it was fun, a kind of game.

And so, lying had become an addiction to him, as it does with many who suffer from personality disorders. He was so good at it that he could lie with a straight face, make eye contact and never blink, where the average prevaricator would look away.

The behavior had become isolating for him as he sank into the mire of falsehood that he had created. He couldn't talk to anyone about it. He couldn't brag to them of his skill in lying. Being a liar is a lonely thing.

If he made a mistake in a lie, he could just make up another lie to cover the problem.

This was different.

There was no room for mistakes, and Mark knew that he was capable of being mistake-prone. Why, after all, wasn't he in medical school? Because he made mistakes, and while not an academic failure, he certainly wasn't destined to spend a lifetime at the pinnacle of the medical world, or even in a local practice like his father.

Mark went back to the apartment to change clothes and to tidy up. It was still before dawn, and he didn't encounter anyone upon his return to Lincoln Street.

When he re-entered the apartment it was a maze of clutter. Boxes from the move were spread around, and the bedroom now looked as if the move had begun with the mattress off the bed. He picked up the large hunting knife that he had used to remove the pillowtop and wiped blood from it, then looked at it, satisfied that it was clean. He put it in the drawer of the bedside nightstand. He hadn't noticed that there was still a trace of blood and some hair attached to the weapon.

Mark now saw that the pillow Lori's head had been

lying on had been left in the apartment. Her blood was still wet and red on the linen. He quickly wadded it into a ball and took it out of the building.

When he returned, he looked for further signs suggesting that there had been foul play in the bedroom. It wasn't that the signs weren't there—they were all around. But Mark Hacking's eyes didn't see them—he was blanking out the evidence of the murder that he had committed.

Neither did he see the blood in Lori's car, a possibility that had so worried him as he had driven to dispose of her body. In fact, Mark was careless, not only missing the blood that was in the car, but in failing to understand that his fresh fingerprints were left on the rear passenger driver's-side door, just like they would be if a person were placing a body in the back seat. Mark Hacking was an amateur killer.

But no thoughts went through his head as he searched the apartment for the evidence that would surely get him in trouble, perhaps into prison, and perhaps, a long shot, but perhaps also cost him his life.

It was a high-stakes game that he had entered. He hadn't planned to kill his wife at first. It had just happened after he continually thought about it over the weekend. In fact, he'd been leading a perfectly content life with her as they prepared for their move to the East Coast. It wasn't as if there was anything particularly wrong with their marriage. There was nothing he could discern before she had caught him in his lie and discovered that he wasn't the person who she had thought that she was married to.

Then she had erupted at him—and he'd snapped.

He had to measure up to his father and brothers, just had to, even if measuring up meant that he would fabricate an imaginary life.

Mark never wondered if his parents, or Lori's, had doubted him. He was just so good telling his stories, lying, even taking the trouble of writing term papers and then asking Thelma to correct them for him. He went to such great lengths to make his creations so believable.

Mark had once traveled to New York for an interview at Columbia University and stayed with Lori's cousin Kathy Black. The night before she had taken him to the campus so he would be able to find his way there from her home. The following morning, he got up, dressed for the interview, left, and in a few hours returned describing the meeting in detail.

Kathy had no reason to suspect that her cousin's husband would lie to her about an interview, much less go to the trouble of creating the intricate details of such a story. He was totally believable to her, she later told Lori's brother Paul. It was preposterous that anyone would even think of questioning what Mark said about his life and his studies, much less actually do it, as Lori had just done. Unthinkable.

The one thing that characterizes the Church is its obsession with family. At the head of that family the man is expected to have a strong presence. That overriding principle is a dominant force in virtually every household. It is supported institutionally by the Church's very structure and the structure of the ladder one must climb to reach the celestial kingdom.

If you are a woman, you just can't get there unless

you are at the side of a man, a man holding the priesthood, but one who honors the priesthood as well.

Herbie had left his den when Mark had exited the apartment with Lori's body. A master of stealth, the cat crept into the living area, hoping for a reassuring pat on the head, but there was nobody there, not even Mark.

The cat sniffed the air, then found specks of blood on the furniture and instinctively knew that they hadn't been there in the past. He lingered, vigilant. Finally, when his curiosity was satisfied, he again crept into the safety of the closet, knowing that Mark was likely to return.

Satisfied that the apartment was in a reasonable enough condition to pass a police inspection, Mark again closed and locked the door to number 7. There was more work to do and the clock was ticking on him.

An idea was beginning to gel in Mark's mind. The more that he thought about it, the more he liked it.

During college, Lori had become a jogger, finding the activity a welcome release from the tension of study, the strain brought on by learning. After their marriage, she continued, running with her pal from Wells Fargo, Elizabeth Read. The two chose one of America's most scenic urban areas to run.

City Creek Canyon lies just to the east of Utah's 1915 State Capitol Building in the heart of downtown Salt Lake City. At its heart is Memory Grove, a memorial area dedicated to Utah's war dead since WWI, and punctuated by the graceful architectural presence of a Greek temple. The two women could have looked at every runners' track in the country and not found a better one than this, right in their own backyard in downtown Salt Lake.

Runner's World magazine dubbed City Creek Canyon and Memory Grove the "Best Urban Run Bar None," a superlative accolade akin to a papal pronouncement in the world of runners. The magazine wrote, "Right behind the stunning state capitol, you can begin a run through Memory Grove/City Creek Canyon, one of the best city-to-nature running segues anywhere. A half-mile and 200 vertical feet after entering Memory Grove (a pleasant little piece of urban greenery), you'll pass through the City Creek Canyon gate, where you can run northeast on a smooth asphalt road, or drop down to a parallel, no bikes allowed, shady creek side single track. From the gate, it's all uphill—3.2 miles (and 700 vertical feet) to the water-treatment plant, and another 2.8 miles (and another 700 vertical feet) to Rotary Park. Ah, but coming back down . . ."

To a non-runner, the trek sounds like agony.

Lori Hacking and Elizabeth Read couldn't have found a better place to jog.

While other urban areas are dangerous places to run, City Creek Canyon is known more for its serenity and less for muggings. Yet there is danger there too. Runners on the trails often see snakes, and the canyon is a habitat to mountain lions, known to attack humans who encroach on their territory.

Mark headed in the direction of the park, turning onto State Street, going past the vast ZCMI Center shopping complex and then up Capitol Hill. To the right was the entrance to the park.

The sun was coming up over Zion.

A thousand thoughts congealed into one: find a plausible reason for Lori's absence. He turned into the park. It was nearly deserted as he slowly eased the car northward along the narrow paved street toward Memory Grove.

He opened the door and put his feet on the ground.

His head was covered with a bandana and he was glad, because a jogger ran past and looked hard at him. She could possibly place him in the park should the police ask her. It was more likely that she had looked at him in apprehension as a woman alone at daybreak in a deserted park might do.

Lori ran in this park almost daily, Mark knew that. He knew that a lone runner in a city park was vulnerable, demonstrated by the passerby who had just seen him. Almost anything could happen to a woman jogging alone, especially a woman as small as Lori.

If he told the family that Lori hadn't come back from her morning run, who would question it?

Mark had a fabulous relationship with his in-laws. Both Thelma and Eraldo Soares were willing to tell anyone who asked that he was the perfect husband for their daughter. He could count on both of them to accept his story, if he chose to tell it. His own family would accept anything that he said as well. Right now, he was the apple of their eye, another son who had graduated from the university with honors and who was now setting out for medical school. He would bring honor to the Hacking name. With Lori, he would bring fine children into the family as well.

The more Mark thought about it, the more he liked the idea of Lori going missing in City Creek Canyon. The area was dense with shrubbery, a perfect place for an assailant to hide, either human or animal.

Mark eased himself back into Lori's car, turned on the ignition, and drove to a parking area across from Memory Grove. The park was still deserted. He came to a stop in front of the home of Nancy Becker, abandoning the car as if Lori had parked it there for a quick morning jog. The time was 5:30 a.m.

He looked the car over one last time, his eyes blind to the bloodstains that a veteran district attorney would soon call evidence.

Mark Hacking walked along State Street among the early birds determined to be the first to hit the office on a Monday morning. They came from near town, Murray, Sandy, West Jordon, Draper Lehi, American Fork, Lindon Orem, and Bountiful. A few came from Layton, Farmington, and Roy. Salt Lake City has perhaps the most desirable work force in the entire country. The population has a work ethic instilled in them since the pioneer days when work meant survival in the harsh environment of early Zion.

It was these industrious souls whom Mark walked among as he made his way back to the apartment on Lincoln. On another day, Lori would have been among them. Yet Lori was in another place now, her body laying in a heap in a Dumpster on the University of Utah campus.

Mark knew that the next few days would be rough. He thought about how to handle the situation as he walked. The answers were hard in coming. He had never killed a person before. It was one thing to be a masterful liar, the king of liars, in fact. It was quite another to be a cold-blooded killer. This was all new to him, and he wasn't sure he liked it. He was still angry with Lori. He had been totally confident in the lies he'd told her. He'd never given a thought to the possibility that she would take matters into her own hands and call the North Carolina school.

What a fool he had been about that, Mark thought, clenching his fists, and again searching them for telltale signs of murder.

It was now barely 6 a.m. What would be the logical period of time to wait to make the call? How long does a husband worry about a missing wife before worry turns to fear? Should he call Lori's work first? How about calling a family member? Was that the logical thing to do? When should he call the police? Who should he call first? There were so many questions that he needed to sort though before making his next move.

There were other things that had to be done. He needed to go over the apartment again in broad daylight to make sure that he hadn't missed any bloodstains.

When Mark reached the apartment building, nobody had yet stirred, from the looks of things. He stuck his key in the door and opened it. He walked into the bedroom and was briefly shocked. The bed now lay bare, with only the box springs visible. The apartment was as he had left it. Boxes were still strewn around in anticipation of the move.

That was it. He needed to buy a mattress, and do it immediately. The absence of a complete bed would be difficult to explain. Besides, he needed something to sleep upon later when he could finally get some rest.

Thus far, Mark hadn't rested. He was running on adrenaline. His body was consumed by excitement—and increasingly, fear.

What if it didn't work?

What if he slipped up as he had a few days before when he was asked something at work about his studies? He had blundered an answer, and had done it while somebody had a video camera pointed at him. He'd quickly corrected himself. It was just small talk, yet he had been hot-wired to perform, to show just how accomplished he was.

That happened more often than Mark liked to admit, even to himself. He wasn't a perfect liar, but he was damned good. Yet there was no room for imperfections now. He had to have his story down pat, flawless, impenetrable. There was no room for even the slightest error, because the consequences were too great.

There was a fall-back position, there had to be. Suddenly it came to him. If things began looking bad for him, he could feign insanity. He had certainly seen enough of it working in a psychiatric hospital.

If he just acted crazy enough, would a jury believe that he had killed his wife in a fit of irrational behavior?

Possibly.

Across town, Chad and Lesa Downs awoke for another Monday in the furniture business. They had owned Bradley's Sleep Etc. for fourteen years and were no longer young entrepreneurs, but veteran business people who knew how to please customers, and please them well.

They'd transformed the place from an average bed shop into a tasteful, full-service furniture store with a Western flair. Hand-crafted deer-antler chandeliers hung from the ceiling. Ranch-style furniture dotted the showroom floor, furniture that could easily belong in the home of even the snottiest Texan. The two had exquisite taste in the stock that they sold, and the store showed it.

The store occupied a freestanding building just down "Third Street" to the south of the Wasatch brewery. The street was lined with commercial enterprises more in line with the tastes of a blue-collar clientele than the upscale market the Downs hoped to attract.

The two look younger than their years, an attractive couple wise in the ways of the furniture business.

Every day in retail is a new adventure, veterans of the business say. You never know who is going to walk through the front door. Sometimes it is a celebrity. Most of the time it is just an average citizen, but on rare occasions, it's a killer. If you are lucky, you aren't the intended victim.

Chad and Lesa opened the store at 9 a.m. Hopefully, sales would be brisk this week before the summer doldrums set in and people began to spend money on school clothes for the kids instead of furniture. With luck, there would be another week or so of good sales, and then there would be a slight fall-off.

Seven employees in the Bradleys' Sleep Shop were a lot of mouths to feed, and Chad and Lesa dreaded the inevitable lulls that came from time to time. When a customer walked through the door on a Monday, that customer was precious, someone to be cherished, someone to be sold.

Mark Hacking came through the front door and walked about twenty feet inside the shop. He was tall, a big man with a shaved head and a closely cropped goatee and mustache. The beard was red, yet his eyebrows were blond, almost disappearing into the forehead, which went on forever. Chad and Lesa looked at him as he stood there awkwardly, as if he couldn't find something that he was looking for.

"He had a deer-in-the-headlights look," Chad remembers.

"He had on a very, very clean white T-shirt," Lesa says. "I had just done my son's laundry and I thought, How can I get my son's clothes that white?"

The two waited at their side-by-side desks. Chad, ever the salesman, sized his customer up. It was difficult.

"He was quiet, but focused, and I thought, Boy, I'm going to have trouble reading him," he recalls.

But the customer wasn't nervous as he looked about the store and waited for sales help.

"I'd like to see a mattress," he said.

"Right this way," the owner said as he had done thousands of times before to thousands of customers.

But this one was different, he remembers now.

"He didn't look like your typical Mormon boy who comes in here," Chad recalls. "They don't come in with goatees and shaved heads."

Chad led him to the mattress department and Mark looked it over, quickly picking one.

"He didn't lie down on the mattress," Chad remembers. "I did think it was strange that he didn't lie down, because lots of guys do that, because their wives just tell them to go out and buy a mattress."

Chad explained to Mark that Bradley's sold two types of mattresses, one more expensive than the other.

"Pillowtops sag," he said. "We sell latex ones as well, but they are more expensive. They don't get body impressions."

"Oh, I don't want that," Mark Hacking said.

Mark dialed the work number of his mother-in-law, Thelma Soares. It was 10:30 a.m. He told her that Lori had gone jogging near Memory Grove and had not come home.

Chapter Six

Across town, the workers at the law office of Gilbert Athay made their way into their building. It was on a corner across the street from the courthouse and just a block away from the *Deseret Morning News* building. Athay's office was in the middle of everything in Utah's capital city. That was as it should be.

Gilbert Athay is one of Salt Lake's "A" list lawyers: someone you go to if you are in trouble with the law and have the funds to pay his fee.

A 1967 graduate of the University of Utah School of Law, Athay has had plenty of time to hone his considerable legal skills.

In 1976, he even flirted with politics. He ran as a Democrat for attorney general against a man who would later become known as a wild card in Utah politics, Robert Hanson. Athay lost.

Since then, he had never done anything but practice criminal law. In Martindale-Hubble, the reference bible to members of the profession, he has a listing with simply his name, address, and phone number. There is no impressive list of clients or victories in the courtroom, just the simple listing. He doesn't afford his fellow lawyers so much as a jot or tittle about his success rate or the famous cases he's tried. Like all lawyers, he was taught not to give the opposition anything. Athay took this advice to heart with a vengeance.

Yet the diminutive lawyer is well liked by other members of the bar, respected for his victories and his sometimes flamboyant courtroom style. Athay is capable of putting on a show and even challenging a judge who he thinks is wrong.

In recent years, courthouse insiders say, Athay had shied away from trying cases, advising his many clients to accept plea bargains. In Utah, murderers face a mandatory minimum sentence of 5 years to life. Rather than risk the vengeance of a jury, Athay, like many prudent lawyers, will arrange a deal for his clients, generally young people with the rest of their lives before them. He will advise a client to take an offer of, say, 5 to 30 years that the DA dangles in front of them. Unless the case is almost slam-dunk winnable, prudent advice might be, "You have a life ahead of you. You have never been in trouble before. Go on up there and keep your nose clean. Be a model prisoner. You will come up for parole in five years. The parole board might look kindly on you. You are twenty-nine now. You can get out in five years. You will be thirty-four. There will be plenty of time for you to make a new life for yourself. Do this for yourself, and do this for your parents. This is hard on them too."

Athay has kept a broad client list over his thirty-eight-year career, representing athletes, politicians, and death row inmates. In 1989, he and two other crackerjack lawyers formed the Rocky Mountain Defense

Fund, a nonprofit agency determined to end capital punishment in the Beehive State. The other two staunch death penalty opponents were Salt Lake attorneys Loni DeLand and Ron Yengich.

The fund quickly broadened its reach, representing inmates in Colorado, Wyoming, Idaho, and Nevada, as well as Utah.

Working with the fund, Athay has fought for the lives of some of Utah's worst killers, including Pierre Dale Selby, who tortured and killed three people in an Ogden stereo shop. Ultimately, Athay wasn't successful in saving Selby, who was executed in 1987 after the prominent attorney spent fourteen years trying to save his life on appeal.

Athay's client John Albert Taylor was convicted for raping and then strangling an 11-year-old girl in Washington Terrace. Utah offers the option of dying before a firing squad, and Taylor faced it in 1996.

But Elroy Tillman, who was alleged to have killed a man in 1982, lived to be grateful to his lawyer. His death sentence was vacated in 2003.

Yet the work of a criminal lawyer such as Gilbert Athay isn't always devoted to representing clients charged with abhorrent crimes. A staple of such a lawyer's business, if not its bedrock, is the representation of average people who run afoul of the law committing average crimes.

Athay's career hasn't been devoid of excitement. He once represented a high-rolling racketeer named Glenn Earl Lloyd II, who stole a page from the long successful New York crime boss Vincent "the Chin" Gigante. The Chin eluded prosecution for years by feigning mental incompetence wearing house slippers and a bathrobe on the streets of New York as he shuffled along the sidewalk.

When Lloyd's day in court came on a charge of money laundering, the closer to the courtroom he got, the sicker he apparently became. He was an hour late for the trial, appearing dazed and confused as he shuffled down the corridor wearing Gigante-style house slippers. The usually glib Lloyd bumped walls and curled up on a courthouse bench with a moan and a mumble.

Athay and the defendant's wife appeared outside the courtroom corridor, and the attorney pulled his client to his feet. But Lloyd turned and headed toward his car, his lawyer chasing him. As the two increased the distance between the courtroom and the automobile, Lloyd's pace quickened and his speech miraculously improved. When he got to the parking lot, he quickly jumped into his car, waving a gun at Athay as the attorney and the man's wife ran after him.

Lloyd was captured after a weekend in Las Vegas. He had foolishly checked into the Mirage hotel under his own name.

If you take State Street south from Athay's office, then ease right, then left onto 300 South (3rd St.) you will eventually come to Bradley's Sleep Shop. The store, and the paperwork that goes with a purchase there would prove to be Mark Hacking's, and his lawyer's, biggest nightmare.

Lesa Downs remembered Mark Hacking well. She remembers most of the customers who come into the store.

"He had a belly," she remembered.

Chad too remembered Mark as he appeared that morning in July.

The sale was effortless. Mark bought his new mattress for $500, with few questions. Chad was able to sell him two "high-tech" pillows, pricey at $50 each. At 10:23 a.m., Chad Downs processed Mark's University of Utah credit card. The charges went through without a hitch.

By now, Mark Hacking was experienced at transporting a mattress. However, this time he had professional help load it onto his SUV.

"I tied the mattress on the top of the car," Chad Downs recalled. "I remember looking inside to make sure that Mark had the pillows. Everything looked normal."

So did Mark Hacking.

"He didn't look to me like he was worn out from being up all night," the furniture man remembered.

Another one of his chores was now done. It was time to begin the next one. Mark drove to the apartment, carried the new mattress and pillows inside, then returned to his car and drove to City Creek Canyon.

Mark was now making calls on his cell phone, hard at work to create the illusion that Lori had gone missing on the park's jogging trail. He worked rapidly and steadily. On the phone, his performance was pure theater as the calls went out one after the other to family members, friends, and co-workers.

He parked and began to look for his wife, asking passersby if they had seen her.

Quickly, friends of the couple converged on the park where Mark Hacking stood. They began to knock on doors of people in the neighborhood, asking if residents had seen a woman fitting Lori Hacking's description.

At 10:45 a.m., a Memory Grove resident named Nancy Becker heard a knock on the door from family friends of Lori and Mark. Lori's car was parked in front of her home. Had Nancy seen her jogging? they asked. Had she seen anything unusual?

At 10:49 a.m., Mark Hacking dialed 911. He reported that his wife Lori was missing.

At police headquarters on 200 South, Sgt. Phil Eslinger maintained the watch log. When the call came in that there was a jogger missing in Memory Grove, it was routine: another missing person who would probably turn up sweating bullets after a jog because she hadn't notified somebody where she was going. A veteran officer in the Salt Lake department, Eslinger had seen about all that Zion had to offer when it came to crime. When calls such as this came in to headquarters, it was always a crapshoot as to where the report would end up. In a minority of cases, such reports turned into homicides. This would bear watching.

At 2:03 p.m. KSL radio reported that there was a jogger missing in Memory Grove. At 5:01 p.m., Mark Hacking was speaking to the press, and the station broadcast what he said live.

"It really blows me out of the water to see how many people care and are willing to give so much of themselves . . . usually when she runs in the morning, I go with her. I just didn't today."

• • •

The day started just like any other for veteran H&R
Block employee Lorraine Beasley. It wasn't until late
Monday afternoon that she learned from a television
news program that her friend was missing.

Lorraine Beasley had stayed in touch with Lori
Hacking after the two had worked together at the H&R
Block tax office in Holladay, a suburb of Salt Lake
City just below the Mount Olympus Wilderness Area.
Lori was moonlighting at the suggestion of a friend
from her business school days.

From the beginning of their acquaintance, Lorraine
thought of the petite young tax specialist as being one
of the "sweetest people I have ever known." The two
had remained friends after Lori left the firm, making
frequent trips to dinner at T.G.I. Friday's, Chili's and
The Old Spaghetti Factory. The friendship was cemented at one of those dinners when Lorraine men-
tioned that her daughter, Jennifer, was moving to Salt
Lake. The woman was concerned about the move, because there was no man in either her or her daughter's
home to help with the lifting. That evening, on the way
to the parking lot, Lori pulled her aside.

"Here's my home number," she told Lorraine. "Just
give me a call when she gets here and Mark and I will
come help."

"Are you sure that will be okay with Mark?" the tax
lady said.

"Oh sure, he likes doing things like that," Lori assured her.

The day Jennifer arrived driving a U-Haul truck,
Lorraine called her friend, not knowing what to expect.

"You know how it is, people tell you that they will do something, then don't really mean it. They seem to have something else to do when you call. Not Lori. She said, 'We'll be right there.'

"They came all the way to South Jordan," Lorraine remembers. "They helped us move everything into the garage. I thought it was nice of Lori to come all the way down from Salt Lake."

Lori brought her hulking husband with her for the move. Lorraine thought he was an "okay guy," but a little strange by her standards.

"What struck me as odd is that he was wearing his scrubs," she remembers. "I worked for an ophthalmologist for twenty-five years and I never saw them wear their scrubs outside the hospital."

Many young employees at university hospitals wear scrubs as a matter of comfort, unconcerned about their appearance.

A week and a half before Lori went missing, Lorraine had "the girls" over for pizza.

"I called over there on a Sunday morning about the dinner and talked to Lori," Lorraine remembers now. "I asked if I was bothering her, because I knew that she was active in the Church."

"No, our ward meets later on Sunday mornings," she told her friend.

The night of the dinner arrived and Lorraine made preparations to entertain her girlfriends.

"I made a special salad," she remembers. "We had cheesecake, but I didn't make it.

"She [Lori] was telling me of their move to North Carolina and all the schools that they'd applied for, and then she was telling me that she was pregnant."

Lori gave her the new address in Carrboro, NC, as well as a new cell phone number.

Lori's pregnancy, her first, was in keeping with the Utah and Mormon tradition of large families. If anything, it was surprising that she and Mark hadn't started their family earlier in their marriage, considering the statistics the faithful have racked up in the state.

The week before Lori went missing, Lorraine checked her mail. In it was a note from Lori:

> Lorraine, thank you very much for inviting me to your home. I had a wonderful time and appreciated your hospitality. I'm going to miss our frequent dinners, but I'm sure glad we were able to get together before I leave. I promise to stay in touch.

When she heard that her friend was missing on the Monday newscast, Lorraine instantly sensed that something had gone terribly wrong.

She called her friend and co-worker, Grace Hanson, who had also just heard the news on television.

Intuitively she told her friend, "I think that they had a blow-up and he accidentally did something to her."

The fact that the woman had gone missing in City Creek Canyon didn't register to Bob Stott at all. The lawyer's mind was filled with other, more pressing things. At 60, the veteran prosecutor and father of six children had seen it all. Away from the hectic pace of the office, he lives a quiet life in a brand-new house in Bountiful. There, gulls that make their home at the Great Salt Lake are a frequent sight, sea birds far away from any ocean.

Away from the courthouse, Stott is a bookworm, reading mostly history and biography. Five of his children are married and one still lives at home with him and his wife, Deanie.

When he doesn't have his nose buried in a book, he rides his motorcycle in the mountains that begin just a few hundred yards from his home.

He also relishes the summer each year and cherishes an annual trip to southern Utah where he and the guys ride trail bikes.

Stott is a son of Utah, born a month after Americans stormed the beaches at Normandy. After high school, he did missionary work in the blistering Texas heat in that state's most sweltering city, Houston. He returned to Utah and received a BA from Brigham Young University in 1968, and a law degree from the University of Utah Law School three years later.

He has spent a lifetime as a stalwart member of the Mormon Church. Each Sunday, he and Deanie can be found teaching Sunday school to juvenile inmates at the Farmington Bay Detention Center for Davis County.

"During the week, I prosecute the fathers and uncles of those to whom I teach religion on Sunday," he quipped.

For twenty-nine years, he has put the state's criminals in the big penitentiary just down I-15 from Salt Lake

City, some for life, and a few for death before a firing squad. During his decades as a prosecutor, Stott has been associated with some of Utah's most infamous cases.

Early in his career Stott was introduced to consummate evil in the person of Ted Bundy. The second-year University of Utah law student, who moonlighted as a serial killer, was prosecuted in Salt Lake for kidnapping after an alert off-duty highway patrolman captured him.

The county's homicide team had spent months trying to sort out the disappearance of young girls in the nearby Wasatch Mountains. After Bundy's 1975 capture, two victims who he'd tried unsuccessfully to abduct picked the personable and presentable murderer out of a line-up, and he was charged and tried for attempted kidnapping.

David Yocom, Salt Lake's current district attorney, had prosecuted the case with the assistance of a new lawyer in the office—Bob Stott. Bundy was found guilty and received a sentence of up to 15 years in prison, frustrating prosecutors who believed he was a murderer, but couldn't put together a case against him.

Just before his 1989 death in the Florida electric chair, Bundy confessed to thirty murders. There may have been as many as 100 nationwide. Bundy's Utah conviction bought time for prosecutors in Colorado who were near nailing their own case against him. When they were ready, they pounced, and Utah extradited Bundy across the Rocky Mountains to a jail cell in Colorado. The Utah case had served a valuable purpose. It kept Bundy locked up until prosecutors in the neighboring state were ready to charge him.

Utah killers are special. No other state quite matches Zion. In fact, no other state even comes close. Stott encountered one of Utah's most colorful, and vicious, murderers when he prosecuted Ervil LeBaron, the patriarch of the deadly Church of the Lamb of God polygamous cult, a Mormon offshoot with roots going back to the nineteenth century. The cult killed more than twenty people, mostly rival prophets and its own family members over a twenty-year period.

LeBaron even had his own daughter strangled because she "hollered a lot" and complained too much, threatening to turn her murderous father in to the police.

Many of the murders were believed to have followed the old Mormon practice of blood atonement.

Ervil LeBaron died in 1981 in prison, where Stott's successful prosecution had landed him. The cult's murders continued unabated for years despite its prophet's death.

The next high-profile defendant prosecuted by Stott aroused deep feelings in Salt Lake City's small minority community. Joseph Paul Franklin, an avowed racist, killed two young black joggers, Ted Fields and Dave Martin, who were running with white women in Liberty Park. The 1981 jury hung on the death penalty, and as a compromise, they agreed to give Franklin two consecutive life terms.

Stott was frustrated by the decision, saying, "In the past fifteen years, we've never had a . . . case that we spent as much effort in trying to obtain the death penalty [for] as in the Franklin case."

The prosecutor says that members of his team

received death threats from white supremacist groups.

"We vigorously sought the death penalty because we felt that Franklin should receive the most severe punishment for his crime. It was a cold-blooded sniper murder of two innocent victims."

Stott's mind would come back to the Franklin case in the coming days as he became aware of a missing jogger in City Creek Canyon.

"[In Franklin] there were no eyewitnesses, no fingerprints, no smoking gun. It was a circumstantial case," he remembered.

"What we learned from the Franklin case—and other capital homicide cases since—is that the single most important factor in a death case is not race or politics, but the strength of the evidence. Only when the case has uncontested physical evidence or a confession will juries seek death."

This knowledge would play an important role in the fate of Mark Hacking. It didn't save another Utah man with a bright future when Stott took former Eagle Scout, honor student, and Mormon missionary Arthur Gary Bishop to trial, and ultimately to his death by lethal injection.

He had killed five boys, each while in a sex-induced frenzy sometimes culminating in necrophilia. Bishop was a pedophile of the first order, luring his victims, two as young as four, with promises of camping trips. He was daring as well, abducting one child from his grandfather's side in a supermarket.

Bishop, an accountant, was also convicted of embezzlement and was eventually excommunicated from the Mormon Church.

In his trial, when Stott played his taped confession, Bishop mimicked the dying words of the children he killed in a falsetto. His fate was sealed when he said on tape, "I'm glad they caught me, because I'd do it again."

Bishop, a deeply religious cradle Mormon, was familiar with the doctrine of blood atonement as preached by early leaders of the Church. He established a friendship with a prison chaplain on death row and asked frequently about giving his own life for the blood that he had shed. He was told that he couldn't.

The former Eagle Scout and Mormon missionary waived appeal and was executed by lethal injection on June 9, 1988. Seven leather straps bound Bishop to the tan gurney. Fear was etched on his face as the lethal chemicals worked their magic.

Five times he had killed children brutally, using a hammer, a pistol, and his bare hands.

Bob Stott had another notch etched permanently on his belt.

It is unusual for a prosecutor to be at the scene of a crime or at the point of arrest, but Ronnie Lee Gardner got his introduction to the prosecutor literally on the courthouse steps.

Gardner was a notorious Salt Lake criminal who had escaped or attempted to escape from prison on numerous occasions. During two different escapes he had killed two people and seriously wounded two others. By 1984, Utah had had its fill of Ronnie Lee Gardner and charged him with the murder of a bartender he'd killed during a robbery.

Re-captured, state prison guards transported him to

the Salt Lake City courthouse for a hearing, entering the building through the basement. But Gardner was more crafty than his keepers and planned yet another escape, having two female friends hide a gun under the water fountain next to the basement's elevators.

Handcuffed, he grabbed the gun and fired at the guards, who returned fire as they retreated into the building's parking area.

Meanwhile, Gardner was still inside the building. He sought escape and blundered into a file storage area near the elevators where two attorneys were ordering files. The lawyers were crouched behind the doorway after hearing the commotion outside. Gardner walked up to them and fired twice at point-blank range, killing one of them.

The convict had been hit by one of his prison guards' bullets as they retreated to the parking lot. He now retraced his steps and hobbled up the stairway of the basement to the first floor.

Meanwhile a bailiff who had heard the shots was coming downstairs looking for his judge, concerned for his safety. Gardner shot and wounded him, and the man died of complications from the injury several years later.

Gardner managed to get outside, escaping the building through a side door. However, he knew quickly that the game was up when he found his gun was out of bullets and he would die shortly unless he surrendered. Injured, and with no weapon, he limped to the front of the courthouse, sat down and waited to be arrested.

Stott heard sirens and commotion as he came down a

stairwell in his office building across the street with his friend Mike George, the investigator on the Gardner case. Instinctively, he knew that his prisoner had caused the action.

"That's Ronnie, he's escaped," he told George.

"We ran out of our office and saw him across the street in a bloodstained white prison uniform surrounded by police," he remembers.

"In October of '85, we tried, convicted, and obtained the death penalty for Gardner for those events," he said.

The case of Ronnie Lee Gardner remains on appeal as it winds through the federal court system on habeas corpus.

Although Gardner was on death row, his violent nature was unabated. He tried to kill a fellow prisoner with a homemade shank.

In another famous case, forger and murderer Mark Hoffman's wife, Dorie, was described as a male-worshipping Mormon wife who never questioned her husband about why he spent so much time in the basement of their home. Her lapsed Mormon husband was using the space to perpetrate forgeries of fake historical documents that he would ultimately sell to Church leaders, including the revered LDS president and prophet Gordon B. Hinckley.

Hoffman knew that there were skeletons in the Mormon closet. Authentic LDS history is far murkier than the official version. He also knew the Church was interested in acquiring potentially embarrassing documents so they could suppress them.

Hoffman, an opportunist, saw a buck to be made, and made it, playing upon the desire of many Mormons to know about their often exciting and colorful history, and in some cases to sweep it away from public view.

At least one Mormon, Gary Sheets, was not as gullible as the hierarchy who bought a steady stream of documents from Hoffman, including the now famous Salamander letter, in which it was purported that Church founder Joseph Smith had come upon a talking salamander that turned itself into an angel.

The forger believed that he was about to be exposed, and attempted to kill the man with a bomb, but succeeded in blowing up his wife and her girlfriend instead.

Stott prosecuted the case, which attracted a flurry of nationwide publicity, most of it unfavorable to the Church. Again the prosecutor found himself in the glare of the spotlight working on a case attracting national attention.

Hoffman was charged with two murders and several counts of fraud. He pled guilty to the two counts of murder and two counts of fraud and admitted that all of the documents were forgeries.

He was sentenced to a 1-to-5-years–to–life sentence, and three 1-to-15-year sentences to run concurrently. The Utah parole board has thus far refused to give him a hearing date. Ron Yengich represented him.

The case was the subject of a best-selling book, *The Mormon Murders* by Steven Naifeh and Gregory White Smith. In it, the authors savaged Stott, portraying him as obediently following the marching orders of Hinckley and the hierarchy of the Mormon Church in sweeping the case under a rug with a plea.

In the book the authors make much of secret Mormon archives. Stott denies that such archives exist and vehemently challenges the assertion that he was marching to a tune whistled by Mormon president and prophet Gordon Hinckley.

"I was only in his office once," he says.

Chapter Seven

Memory Grove began to fill, as word was passed in the close-knit Salt Lake community that a jogger had gone missing. The curious and the determined both came.

It had begun when three of Lori's co-workers came to the park after a curious phone call to her office alerted them that she was perhaps missing. Mark had arrived in his Dodge Durango, quickly telling them that he had called police to tell them that Lori was gone.

Curiously, they noted, he called police again to report her missing. Mark was distraught, they thought.

They would describe his next actions as an "aimless search," walking off from them, pondering. He then returned to the truck and placed an address book in his lap. Mark Hacking began to call relatives to tell them that Lori was missing, using not only his cell phone, but Lori's as well.

Meanwhile, the search grew, ever so slightly at first, a stream of Good Samaritans coming to the park. As the week went on, it would become a torrent. The curious watched from a respectful distance as police spoke with a large 29-year-old man with a goatee and shaved head. He could have been one of their own, so similar in appearance was he to some Utah police and correctional officers who assumed the tough-guy image.

The image had come about shortly after Mark and Lori got married. It was not done because he wanted to look menacing—Mark's bushy head of red hair was thinning and he'd shaved his head out of vanity.

The look-alike appearance to some in law enforcement wasn't helping Mark Hacking. As Lori's determined co-workers looked along the trail and into the scrub bushes lining the narrow canyon cut through its steep walls, the cops were taking a hard look at a man who might be a suspect.

The weather can get hot, even in nearly mile-high Salt Lake City. The town was enjoying a typically sunny summer period. Searchers were dressed for the temperature, casual and cool.

The people of Salt Lake, and all of Utah, are accustomed to searches. Each year, a handful of adventurers get lost in the backcountry. Some fall victim to avalanches, the mountains' most sure and deadly killer. Others get separated from a group, become disoriented, and fall victim to the mountain chill that is inevitable at higher elevations after sunset. Still others venture out alone and never are heard of again.

Two years before, 14-year-old Elizabeth Smart had been taken from her home at gunpoint. Her sister Mary Katherine told her parents of the abduction. The following day, June 6, 2002, the foothills above Salt Lake City, and above the Smart home, swarmed with hundreds of volunteer searchers. Police were deluged with more than 100 tips. Days turned into weeks and months and seemingly everyone in the region continued to cast an eye for the missing teenager. Nine months later, the girl was found alive with her alleged abductors, an itinerant street preacher and "prophet" named Brian David Mitchell, who called himself Emmanuel, and his "wife," Wanda Ilene Barzee.

As word spread through Salt Lake, acquaintances of Lori Hacking and total strangers descended upon the canyon. Eventually, the number of volunteers searching for her swelled to upwards of 1,000.

It was a made-for-media event. Television loves crowds, drama, and pathos. When Lori vanished without a trace, TV news crews kicked into high gear, telling the story of the attractive jogger who was missing. Soon they trained their cameras on her husband, who was more than obliging when it came to granting an interview.

By Tuesday morning, Salt Lake media knew that they had a story, and the city's network affiliates began to drift into the canyon. In the early afternoon, veteran KSL radio reporter Ben Winslow arrived.

Soon, Salt Lake police volunteer coordinators arrived to help liaison between the searchers and the cops. As a longtime street reporter, Winslow knew the faces. Eventually, veteran SLPD spokesman Detective Dwayne Baird came on the scene to handle the media.

Mark Hacking wasn't on the scene, however, and the media found its first viable news story with the arrival of Lori's mother, Thelma Soares. The quiet, dignified woman would be thrust into the media spotlight as a symbol of what was to become a tragedy.

Paul Soares first learned of his sister's disappearance from his stepmother, Jana.

"She told me Lori went jogging and hadn't come back," he remembered.

Paul called Mark, whom he had seen only a couple of weeks prior on July 4.

"What's going on?" he asked.

"His tone of voice was nervous, but worried," Paul later said. "There were no red flags though."

Paul was unaware of any strange behavior on the part of his brother-in-law. He didn't know that Mark was now smoking and drinking. He didn't believe Lori knew either.

"She wouldn't have put up with that," he said later, certainty in his voice.

The national media had arrived in the early afternoon, building its satellite city around the news event. They always look the same. Television, the dominant medium for the past fifty years, has refined the way it covers events to a precise and predictable art. But behind its well-coiffed reporters with sonorous voices, their world is filled with gritty producers and technicians, constantly on cellular phones or thumbing Black-Berrys in contact with their networks' headquarters in New York, Los Angeles, or Atlanta.

The crews that travel the country following sensational murders and hurricanes now briefly made Salt Lake their home. These veterans of mayhem and natural disasters are masters at putting meat on the bones of misfortune. They clamored for sound bites from any player who could contribute, and they got them.

Thelma's arrival was exactly what the networks wanted for the evening's newscast. She was presentable and articulate, exuding pathos—just the image to provoke empathy in millions of households nationwide.

Many people, when confronted with the intrusive snout of a television camera thrust into the face, are intimidated. Thelma Soares was a natural, despite her desperate worry.

Television crews from across the country descended upon Zion to feed the ravenous hunger of the nation's twenty-four-hour news cycle. The beautiful Lori Hacking, now missing, was far more appealing to the average news consumer than George Bush or John Kerry could ever be. Her worried mother would provoke deep feelings in every mother who was tuned in.

The crews knew from experience that she had plenty to be worried about. They had covered countless stories of missing people before, most recently the disappearance of Laci Peterson.

Mark had called the police shortly after arriving at the park. Very quickly after the cops got there and got the Lincoln Street address from him, a radio crackled and a unit was dispatched to the apartment.

The arrival of the bloodhounds of Rocky Mountain Rescue was a made-for-TV moment as well. Everybody loves a dog, and the hounds made good fodder for the network's relentless appetite. But the animals couldn't catch a scent and the fierce summer heat made their work difficult at best.

Others arrived as well.

The crews remembered the last big Salt Lake disappearance that they'd covered.

The news crews remembered Elizabeth Smart and her family—knew them on a first-name basis.

When Elizabeth's uncles, Chris and Dave, showed up to coordinate the search effort, the reporters and producers were delighted. The work was in good hands. To many, the search ethic of the people of Salt Lake City is a Mormon thing, an outgrowth of the cohesiveness of the pioneers who had trudged across a continent to found Zion. With them it was either pull together—or die. In most towns, volunteers search for the missing. In Salt Lake City, they do it on a biblical scale.

A cop stood at the door of Mark and Lori Hacking's apartment when Thelma Soares arrived after leaving the park, worried about Herbie the cat. An animal lover, she had been concerned that Herbie didn't have food and water, and she had asked her friends David and Debra Gehris from her ward to drive her by the apartment to check on him.

She was told by the police officer that she couldn't enter the apartment. He agreed to leave food and water when his shift ended.

The following day, when Thelma checked, the cops told her that the food and water were gone, so the cat must be okay, and hiding.

Lack of sleep was now taking its toll on Mark. He had been up all night, first killing Lori, then disposing of her body, the gun, and the bloody bedding. He had bought the new mattress from that nice store on South 3rd Street and had taken it home. Now a full-scale search for his wife was under way and he was the center attraction. What's more, the cops had taped off his apartment as a crime scene.

In a way, Mark was enjoying himself. He had spent a lifetime turning himself into the life of the party, the funny guy who was the focal point of attraction. Now he had hit a bonanza of attention—but it wasn't attention to his liking. He was having to think on his feet, and he knew that his fatigue-plagued mind could fail him at any point, with disastrous results.

Now, on top of fatigue, he felt fear and dread, compounded with the anger he continued to nurse from the night before. He had to keep up the façade of a worried husband whose faithful wife was missing. Even at this early stage, it was becoming increasingly difficult. The questions were coming from all sides, and he knew that he must repeat the same answers over and over again.

As friends, family, and police surrounded him, Mark began the construction of his story, telling them that he had already run the jogging route that Lori followed.

"When was the last time you saw her?"

"What was she wearing?"

"Does she have any enemies?"

"Do you have any enemies?"

"Were you having problems?"

Mark responded the best he could. God, he was tired.

At approximately 10:07 a.m., July 19, 2004, Mark Hacking called Salt Lake City police and reported that his wife, Lori, had left their apartment to go jogging and never returned. A few minutes later, he'd called Lori's employer and informed her co-workers that he'd located her car in Memory Grove and that he was currently there looking for her. At about 10:46 a.m., Mark again called police and told them the same thing.

Within minutes, police had suspected that in all likelihood, Mark Hacking had killed his wife, never letting on to him anything other than their concern for her well-being and hopes of finding her alive. They quickly obtained a search warrant.

The police located Lori's car on Canyon Road. What they found revealed that the seat was adjusted in such a position that a person of Lori's height could not reach the pedals or steering wheel in order to drive the vehicle. The mirrors were also out of adjustment for a person of Lori's size. Red flags went flying as they quickly calculated the distance from the seat to the pedals for a man of Mark Hacking's height.

When police combed through Mark's SUV, they found a sales receipt from Bradley's Sleep Etc. It showed that Mark had been in the store purchasing a new mattress and pillows at 10:23 a.m. on July 19, 2004.

The quickly impounded both cars as evidence.

At the apartment, the Salt Lake cops hit a jackpot in circumstantial evidence when they found Lori Hacking's purse, containing her wallet and keys. They also noticed that the couple's bed was made up with sheets that had crease marks consistent with having been recently removed from their packaging. They also found several knifes in the drawer of a nightstand next to the bed. One of the knives appeared to contain blood and fibers. Fibers were also observed inside the knife sheath.

For Mark Hacking, now sometimes trembling with fear, it was only a matter of time until the snare being set for him by the police would close.

KSL radio's Ben Winslow would readily tell you, "I'm good at what I do." He didn't lie. With Winslow, such words were not a boast but a statement of fact.

The reporter's boyish looks were deceptive. He was tough and thorough.

Winslow is not the kind of on-air "talent" who makes it through the industry on the weight of a sonorous voice alone—his voice is high-pitched and clipped. It wasn't how he sounded that mattered to KSL, but what he consistently delivered to the station's listeners. A former print reporter who'd made the jump to broadcast, he knew how to dig up a story—how to cultivate sources. In the Salt Lake City Police Department, his sources ran deep. Winslow had repeatedly dusted his competitors in print with shoe leather and contacts. He was about to do it again.

Winslow stood in Memory Grove and looked around at the trickle of journalists coming into the park in search of a story. He knew that in the next few moments he would turn the trickle into a deluge, because he had a scoop.

The reporter looked at a colleague, as he was about to go on the air live to report from the park. "Watch this," he said.

At 4:03 p.m. Ben Winslow told KSL's listeners that police had seized both Mark's and Lori's cars, and had impounded the Dumpster at their apartment complex.

Television crews ran to their satellite trucks. Producers frantically dialed cell phones to their news desks. Print journalists did the same. What had been a routine missing persons story had now turned into something more.

To the public, the story raised a few eyebrows, but little more. To the press, it was a full-blown red flag with trumpets blaring in the background. It was a signal that this story could go big, very big.

Veteran news people, whether in broadcast or print, have savvy about them that the public doesn't possess. Some of them call it "vibes," while others refer to it as news sense. It is a skill that is almost congenital with some journalists. They know when a story is blowing big. The skill is particularly prevalent in reporters who work large markets. It is even more pronounced the higher up the job chain a journalist's career takes him, either as a producer or a reporter. Those with the best news sense, the almost psychic ability to smell out a story, quickly rise to the top of their profession.

Ben Winslow was such a journalist, a radio street reporter whose work is monitored constantly by his colleagues.

If the cops had the car, as Winslow had just reported, then Mark Hacking was a suspect. The press knew that they couldn't report it that way yet, but the revelation was enough to generate a substantial commitment of manpower and news budget to covering Lori's disappearance.

Mark Hacking was a suspect from thirty minutes after police had first arrived at the park, Detective Baird later said.

CSI would soon be going over every possession

Mark and Lori Hacking had touched. They would commit manpower of their own to retracing the steps of the missing person up until the time that she'd lost contact.

Winslow's reporting cemented the local competition's commitment to the story even farther as he reported that the cops had also found what could be evidence of foul play in a Dumpster.

The scramble was on now as reporters from sister station KSL, NBC affiliate KTBX, ABC station KUTV, the CBS outlet, and Fox's KTSU dove into the story headlong. Top reporters from *The Salt Lake Tribune* and the Church-owned *Deseret Morning News* began to dig.

The fact that a comely Mormon woman was missing within blocks of the center of the universe for Mormons, Salt Lake's Temple Square, near the grave of Brigham Young, held something special for the newspaper. She was missing within eyeshot of the state capital. Soon its reporters would find that Lori Hacking had married into a prominent Orem family, and that she and her husband were extremely popular in their neighborhood ward.

While Winslow had his scoop, and would lead others to the story, the *Deseret Morning News* held an edge. The paper, which had been founded by Brigham Young, would make the playing field uneven for other news outlets working the story.

Throughout coverage of the case, journalists from the *Deseret Morning News* got access to family members of Lori and Mark Hacking when other news outlets did not. Why should journalists from the old *Deseret News* and Church-owned KSL get all the leads? As is commonly said in Mormon Utah, "They are one of us." It is a phrase applied to reporters every bit as much as it is applied to politicians scrambling for votes. It is a phrase that permeates every aspect of life in the state.

Mark was busy making and taking phone calls from friends and family members wanting to know if he had heard anything, wanting to know the status of the search, and wanting to do anything they could to help find Lori. He expertly kept up the façade of the worried husband desperate to find his wife.

A media frenzy was building around him. Already, mobile news units were buzzing his Lincoln Street address, getting shots of the gray-trimmed brown brick apartment complex on his tree-lined street.

There was so much, just so much to think about, that he couldn't afford the luxury of sleep, yet he desperately needed it to continue.

Mark instinctively knew that he needed to control the flow of news, every bit as much as he needed to control the search, the police, and his family.

At 10 p.m. he dialed the number of the *Deseret Morning News*. Laura Hancock came on the line. The interview was brief.

Mark hung up the phone to fight off the panic attack that he knew was about to engulf him. He had been there before, and had learned to cope. He even kept a booklet in his locker at work, a primer on how to manage the attacks when they came. . . .

The panic attack was coming big time now. He was thinking of everything, including the locker and what was in it and on it. He was also thinking he was about to be a failure again. Mark just couldn't keep this level of stress up much longer.

What would people think when they looked inside his locker at work?

The outside of the locker held two photos, one of Mark standing outdoors, and the other with another guy. The photos weren't what worried him though. It was the signs he had written and taped to the locker that now bothered him.

"Braney man is in your hands," one said. The other, "Sturdy hard men need help with sex."

If anybody saw those, what conclusions would they draw from them?

As the media gathered in City Creek Canyon and Memory Grove, detectives went to the downtown Wells Fargo office where Lori had worked as a trading assistant.

Co-workers related a strange call from Mark Hacking at 10 a.m. the previous day.

Brandon Hodge, who Lori had been training, answered. Instead of asking to speak with his wife, Mark had asked, "By the way, how is Lori?"

"Well, she's not making it into work yet," Hodge had replied. Lori was never late to work, never. She had been in due at 7 a.m.

Nearby, Lori's supervisor, Randy Church, overheard the conversation and took the phone from Hodge.

"She hasn't returned from jogging in Memory Grove," Hacking told him.

Suddenly, curiosity about an employee who was late to work turned to concern.

"Oh, my God, her [work] clothes are still here," Mark said.

"You need to call police," Church told Mark. "Get off the phone."

But at 10 a.m., Mark Hacking wasn't calling from the couple's apartment. He was busy buying a mattress at Bradley's Sleep Etc.

As the manager told the police about the call, more red flags went up.

They seized Lori's computer to check its e-mail.

Across town, police were calling Chad and Lesa Downs to check out the receipt found in the car, but the two had escaped the sleep shop to go to a ballgame where their kids were playing. When they got home that night, there was a message from their salesman at the store. Lesa returned the call.

"Where have you been?" the employee asked.

"At a ball game with the kids," Lesa answered.

"Police have been calling the store," he continued. "They are looking for a missing woman."

Lesa hung up and dialed the number left by the Salt Lake City detective.

The previous day, police had put out a request that anybody who was in the park the morning of July 19 was to call the police hotline.

Police were on to Mark Hacking from the very beginning. The wheels of justice were now in motion to put the former Mormon missionary into a cell for the rest of his life, or at least as much of his life as Utah law permitted. If possible, they would cause his death by lethal injection or firing squad, whichever he chose. Yet the cops kept quiet about what they believed.

Utah, like scores of other "Red States" had passed a law making the killing of a fetus in the act of murdering the woman who carried it a capital offense, punishable by death. The statutes, pro-choice activists charge, are political in nature, an end-around method of getting a fetus declared a viable human being, a person, even though it is inside the womb. Political pro-life strategists hope that such laws will ultimately find their way to the Supreme Court, and if upheld, make abortion upon demand a thing of the past by defining a fetus as a living human being once and for all. Murder would certainly outweigh a woman's right to privacy in the eyes of justice, making *Roe* a thing of the past. Lori had repeatedly told friends that she was five weeks pregnant. The cops and the district attorney's office would quickly learn this in the course of interviews with those closest to the missing woman. If the body could be found quickly enough, the medical examiner might find an intact fetus.

Salt Lake City cops were busy. They quickly went to the LDS ward house near the Hacking apartment and learned that there was a Dumpster behind the church. What is more, they found that the trash bin was under twenty-four-hour surveillance by a video camera. They seized the tape.

Another Dumpster was under surveillance as well, this one at the Neuropsychiatric Institute on the campus of the University of Utah, Mark Hacking's workplace.

As Mark Hacking was giving interviews to the four Salt Lake network-affiliate television stations, police were already honing in on him as their chief suspect. Yet he wasn't the only one. The usual suspects were rounded up and grilled. Cops questioned known sex offenders whose MOs dovetailed with seizing a female jogger in a park setting, despite the fact that Lori Hacking's blood had already been found, likely linking foul play to her husband.

It was now just a matter of letting Mark Hacking slip up until he fell into the net that was already cast and waiting for him.

Search helicopters hovered over Memory Grove, looking for the missing jogger while exhausted searchers sat on the lawns neighboring the park. Homeowners didn't mind the little trespass. By now, the crowd looking for Lori had swelled to 1,000, with no sign of her.

In the background, a quiet hum announced the presence of satellite trucks, their generators keeping the sophisticated electronics running so that they could be in constant contact with their network hubs in New York, Los Angeles, and Atlanta.

Neighbor Dave Wallace, who lived near the park, took his daughter for a walk amid the throng of journalists, producers, and technicians now covering the story.

All of the commotion in the neighborhood frightened the young girl, and the two quickly returned home.

But, Wallace told reporters, "you didn't hear a lot of complaints."

Detective Kelly Kent, a forty-something veteran of the Salt Lake City homicide squad, now directed the investigation of the presumed murder of Lori Hacking.

An essential skill acquired by police who make it beyond patrolman status is the ability to act. Beat cops learn it well as they come to know the good guys and bad guys in the neighborhoods they patrol. Investigators acquire the ability quickly as they learn and hone the art of the bluff—being able to make a suspect believe that they know more than they actually do. Eventually the skill is developed into a game, the familiar good cop/bad cop interrogatory technique seen on television. But unlike so much that is seen on cop shows, this is real world policing. Kent and her team were ready, more than ready, for anything a penny-ante amateur criminal like Mark Hacking could throw at them.

Chapter Eight

Grace Hanson was worried about her friend Lori Hacking. For three-and-a-half months, Lori had moonlighted at H&R Block, where Hanson worked, trying to ease the financial pinch that she and Mark seemed to find themselves in each month. Grace instantly liked Lori. The two became friends, going to dinner frequently with Lorraine Beasley.

"She knew more about some things a lot better than the rest of us," Grace said, "because she worked in the bank on securities, and when it comes to that part, she was really knowledgeable. She caught on really fast."

Lori's friend Rebecca Lloyd had talked Lori into the job, Grace remembered. Lori was a perfect fit, getting along easily with all of the women who worked in the Cottonwood.

Grace had met Mark at a company banquet and liked him immediately. She was impressed with the way he treated his wife. The two seemed to care so much for each other, although Mark wasn't overly affectionate.

When she heard that Lori Hacking was missing in City Creek Canyon, Grace was genuinely worried that something had gone terribly wrong. She didn't give a thought to the idea that Mark could have hurt Lori. After all, three weeks before, the usually reserved Lori had confided in her.

"I don't feel like she ever opened up," Grace remembers. "She would talk a little bit about what she was doing at the other job, but beyond that, it would be unusual for her to say anything.

"She said, 'I've gone off the pill,'" Grace says. "'I shouldn't be telling you this personal stuff, but I've gone off the pill.'"

She was so excited that she might be pregnant, even the reticent Lori couldn't contain herself.

The Mormon Church had embraced Thelma Soares from the beginning. The Orem woman is active in her ward and much loved. In a faith filled with music, Thelma was music itself, serving her Church as a musical director.

At her side was Windsor Stake President Scott Dunaway. In the LDS Church, the president of a stake is the equivalent of a district manager in the business world. He presides over several wards.

Dunaway worked as assistant dean and director of the Brigham Young University Washington Seminar internship program. He also served on the national advisory board of the LDS Foundation. Scott Dunaway was clearly a man on the way up in the Mormon pecking order, and was quick to show it.

During the search, Dunaway was Thelma Soares' handler, along with fellow ward member David Gehris. The two would shield her from a world that was rapidly making her life its own.

Mormons are nothing if not protective of their own. Initially, Dunaway served as go-between for Thelma and for Mark's parents. As time went by, he only concerned himself with Lori's mother.

In her first appearances before the media, Thelma expressed dismay when questioned whether her son-in-law could have harmed Lori. She told the press how he often came to her home to help her, volunteered to do small jobs for her, a single woman living alone.

Thelma Soares went even further, speaking of how proud she was of Mark, and the fact that he was soon going off to medical school in North Carolina.

At 73, Thelma Soares was self-reliant, still a formidable woman. Her handlers could have stayed home.

Mark Hacking had created a world for himself, a world where he was the center of attention, a brilliant pre-med student following in the heroic footsteps of his brother and father. Over two decades under the same roof with a physician, he had learned the lingo of medicine early and well. He could credibly embellish the lies of his imaginary life.

Now, his greatest fears were coming true as he became increasingly aware that he would not be able to make his plan work.

Had he been sloppy? Deep down he knew he had. In the excitement of the moment, and then suffering from fatigue, he had left loose ends, he was certain.

Had he left blood anywhere? He hadn't seen any, but he didn't see dirt on other things that a woman, or a detective, would notice. Where was the knife? He was chilled that he'd forgotten where he had put it. What had he done with the gun? For that matter, where had he put Lori's body? Was it in the Dumpster at the ward house, or the one at work? Mark's head spun.

There would be questions, Mark knew. The police had not just taken his word that his wife was missing. They had actually come to the apartment and even now were going through his and Lori's things.

The cops' questions were becoming more pointed, more direct, more accusatory. Gone was the man-to-man comfort they had given him at first when he'd acted like a worried husband who feared harm had come to his wife. Gone was the sense that he was a part of the team trying with the police and the searchers to find Lori. Instead, they were beginning to act as if he had done her harm.

Why didn't they believe him?

It didn't matter. He knew that in all likelihood he wouldn't be able to hold up under questioning. Mark might delude others. He didn't delude himself. The cops were going to find out pretty quickly that he had killed his wife. It was only a matter of time. The thought of prison, and worse, now tore at Mark's insides.

What if he acted insane?

Mark had acted almost his entire life. What if he could convince the police and prosecutors that he had killed Lori and didn't know what he was doing because of some psychoses?

He had heard that there was such a thing as an insanity defense. But Mark was unschooled in the law. He didn't know that such a defense was seldom used and extraordinarily difficult to prove. The more he thought about it, the more he liked the idea. He would convince everybody that he was crazy. If he was successful, he'd spend a few months in a cushy mental ward, then convince his doctors that their treatment had worked and he would go free.

Mark began walking. The mountains were silhouettes in the background as he strolled the ever-quiet neighborhoods near downtown.

He was so alone in this new world he had created for himself. He had been able to confide some things in his wife, at least on a limited basis. Now he had nobody to talk to as he weighed his options.

At police headquarters, detectives went over what they had on Mark Hacking at the end of the first day, and on the morning of the second. They were convinced that the man had killed his wife. In fact, they even knew where he had killed her. Forensics would soon establish that it was almost certainly the blood of Lori Hacking they had found in the couple's bedroom.

Yet they didn't have enough to take to Stott in the DA's office. Lori Hacking was missing, and for all the police knew, she might very well never be found. A murder was not a murder without a body. The blood they'd discovered could just as easily have come from a bloody nose hammered during a domestic argument as from a knife or a gun.

There were some promising developments. The cops had contacted local security firms and told them they wanted to see any videos their surveillance cameras had taken of suspicious activities around Dumpsters. One company told them they had a shot of a man dumping something large on the university campus.

Go crazy. He kept coming back to it again and again, increasingly coming to believe that he had been sloppy in the killing and had left evidence that would hang him.

Did Utah still have a firing squad? Mark vaguely knew the name Gary Gilmore, and that he had been at the prison in Draper, the first U.S. execution since the resumption of capital punishment. Mark lived not too far from the old state prison where one of America's most outrageous executions had taken place. Labor activist Joe Hill was killed at what is now a shopping area near a park, which occupies the rest of the old Utah prison site.

Would that be his fate? What did it feel like when the bullets hit the breastbone and tore through it, exploding the heart and severing the backbone?

Terror began to fill him with a dread he had never known before. He had to do something, and he had to do it quickly or he was likely going to spend the next night in the Salt Lake County Jail.

Mark Hacking had retreated into another persona each time he had confronted failure in his life. The lies would save him. Yet no options remained. He could run, but where, and with what money? He could change his appearance, but it would take a long time for his hair to grow out.

He needed a retreat. And he needed a drink to calm

himself. Mark Hacking bought beer and began his binge. Nobody knows where Mark Hacking started drinking that night, but he was found drunk in downtown Salt Lake City.

Alcohol does different things to different people who are not accustomed to it and who are not habitual drinkers. On an empty stomach it is an insidious drug that sneaks up on the unsuspecting rapidly, until they either fall asleep, throw up, or are totally incoherent. Frequently it makes cowards into brave men. Most people are too cowardly to commit suicide, but someone can face death much more easily if he has bolstered himself with alcohol.

Mark reached into his pants for the bottle of pills—barbiturates—that he had brought from the apartment. He gulped them all.

He staggered into the parking lot of a hotel near the business district. Mark reached into his pockets and took out a Palm Pilot. His stylus jabbed at the screen, writing what he hoped were his final words in life.

"This is justice."

The Chase Suite Hotel sits on the corner of a busy street on the eastern fringe of downtown Salt Lake City. It is a favorite of businessmen, Mormons on a pilgrimage to Zion, vacationers on their way to the seven ski resorts that are near the city, and Utes fans because of its proximity to the university. It is a pleasant two-story hotel, boasting a large pool and heated spa. The suites are large and airy, even offering fireplaces.

Mark removed all of his clothes, then put his sandals back on. There, standing butt naked on the asphalt outside a strange hotel he began to scream and run wildly in the parking lot.

He did not check in.

When a call comes in to dispatch at the Salt Lake City Police Department that a fully grown man is running naked in a hotel parking lot, the immediate supposition runs in two directions: The subject is either under the influence of drugs or alcohol, or he is in need of psychiatric attention. Not so when police arrived and found that the man creating the disturbance at 2 a.m. was Mark Hacking.

The police were one step ahead of the novice criminal, according to Salt Lake City Detective Dwayne Baird.

"We knew what he was doing and turned him over to his brother."

The cops weren't ready to make an arrest yet. They didn't even have a body, and when the charge is to be murder, that is almost essential.

Mark Hacking was checked in to the University of Utah psychiatric unit for observation. He was now where he wanted to be, safe in an institutional setting of and not far from his workplace. Most importantly, he was not in the county jail.

And for a time at least, Lori's relatives, as well as his own, would be held at arm's length by the staff.

At last Mark could get some rest. He would have time now to think things through without the glare of television cameras dogging his every move as they had done at the park. He would be under the care of medical professionals, whom he was so accustomed to dealing with. His only visitors would be family members.

Mark harbored little doubt that he could convince the shrinks who worked there that he had killed Lori while he was mentally imbalanced. In his work at the hospital, he had watched patients, the way they spoke, the way they joked, the way they cried, the way they retreated into themselves, the way they sometimes manipulated their keepers. He knew all the moves.

He was again in the world of his own making, the world where he could create any persona he liked and get away with it. A world where Mark Hacking was firmly in control.

Mark became increasingly convinced that mental illness was a defense for him as tight as the skin of a sausage.

The world would find sympathy for poor Mark Hacking, the unfortunate one, the man who was on the road to success when mental illness destroyed his life, his wife, and his future.

He would walk.

Mark coiled up on his hospital bed and went to sleep.

Word spread around City Creek Canyon that Mark Hacking had been taken to the hospital after being picked up naked by police in a hotel parking lot. Reporters scrambled, calling the Chase Suite Hotel for confirmation. It didn't take them long to find out the truth from his own family members, who corroborated that Mark was now a patient in the psych unit of the University of Utah Medical Center.

This was no longer simply a story of a jogger missing in a scenic Utah canyon. It was big national news.
The 24-hour news cycle could now be fed for days,
maybe weeks on end.

Only the greenest rookies among the media now believed that they were covering a simple disappearance.
The veteran journalists instinctively knew that they
were dealing with murder, and that the husband of the
deceased was the likely killer. Reporters' suppositions
turned into near certainty that they were at the epicenter of a story that would rival the disappearance of Laci
Peterson, the Clara Harris case, the Andrea Yates case,
and even O. J. Simpson.

The road warriors who follow such things for the
networks began looking for good restaurants and bars
in Salt Lake City to help break up the monotony of the
stake-out that could last weeks. These veterans of the
darker side of the news business knew one thing and
knew it well: If their professional duties called them to
a strange city for days and weeks on end, they should
live well and enjoy the down time, what little there was
of it. What's more, the expense accounts were ample
enough for them to live in a lifestyle on the road that
would be the envy of anyone in any other business.

They knew that as Mark Hacking relaxed in the
comfort of the university's psych hospital, the net of
evidence would begin to close around him. Crime-lab
experts would bring the science of modern policing
into the apartment.

What the journalists didn't know was that it wasn't
difficult for the police to gather evidence. Lori's luxuriant dark hair was everywhere. Long strands, unnotice-

Mark Hacking's jail photo.

Thelma Soares was a pillar of her church. Her world was filled with music until the death of her daughter, Lori. *Steven Long*

Lori's father, Eraldo Soares, speaks to reporters in the Salt Lake City courthouse after Mark Hacking pleaded guilty. His eloquence and fury moved many close to the case. *Steven Long*

Paul Soares, Lori's older brother. *Steven Long*

The Mormon Temple in Bountiful, Utah, where Mark and Lori Hacking were married. *Steven Long*

The Hackings' apartment building at 127 South Lincoln. *Steven Long*

Mark and Lori's apartment was only a half a block from their Ward House. Police found evidence from the murder in the garbage behind the building. *Steven Long*

Mark Hacking reported to family, friends, and the Salt Lake City cops that his wife had gone jogging in Memory Grove and City Creek Canyon. *Steven Long*

The Dumpster behind Mark's workplace at the University of Utah Neuropsychiatric Institute. Many believed he deposited Lori's body there. *Steven Long*

Mark Hacking walked into this convenience store to buy cigarettes right after the murder; on a security camera he appeared to be looking for blood on his hands. *Steven Long*

Chad and Lesa Downs outside their furniture store on 300 South. They sold a new mattress to Mark Hacking after the murder. *Steven Long*

MISSING
FROM CITY CREEK CANYON MEMORY GROVE AREA SALT LAKE CITY UTAH - JULY 19, 2004

LORI HACKING
27 YEARS OLD - 5'3" - 115 LBS - HAZEL EYES
DARK BROWN HAIR - DARK COMPLEXION
PLEASE CONTACT SLC POLICE: (801) 799-3000
WITH ANY INFORMATION - www.findlori.com

During the search, friends distributed hand-bills with a picture of Lori that would become familiar to the nation.

KSL Radio's Ben Winslow scored a series of scoops on the disappearance of Lori Hacking. *Steven Long*

The entrance to the Salt Lake Valley Solid Waste Facility,
where what was left of the body of Lori Hacking
was found. *Steven Long*

The Salt Lake City Police diggers endured heat, odors, insects,
and boredom searching for Lori's remains. *Steven Long*

The Duchesne County Cadaver Dog team is nationally known for their skill in finding dead bodies. *Duchesne County Sheriff's Department*

Sgt. J. R. Nelson turned over a trash bag with his rake and instantly recognized Lori Hacking's hair. *Steven Long*

Bob Stott would lead the prosecution of Mark Hacking. He knew from the beginning that there would never be a trial. *Steven Long*

Salt Lake County
District Attorney
David Yokom.
Steven Long

The courtroom of Judge Denise Lindberg. *Steven Long*

The grave of Lori Soares Hacking, in an Orem cemetery at the base of the Wasatch Mountains. *Steven Long*

After Mark was charged with murder, Lori's father had her married name removed from the tombstone. A Portuguese word, *Filhinha*, meaning "little daughter," replaced it. *Steven Long*

able to the layman, were quickly spotted by the forensics experts who now scrutinized the space for even the most minute clues.

Hair wasn't the only evidence they found. Mark had been sloppy when it came to cleaning up the aftermath of murder. Lori's blood was there on the nightstand, evidence that could be matched with the DNA samples from the hair that she had casually and unknowingly shed in life.

In addition to their work in the apartment, SLC detectives were making calls, backtracking Mark's and Lori's every move for the last week.

The cops had easily found a Bradley's Sleep Etc. bill of sale in Lori's car.

Mark Hacking was so stupid, they thought. It was dated the day that he'd reported his wife missing. Moreover, a brand-new mattress was on the bed. And the day after the murder, while searching the Dumpster in the church parking lot, a mattress had been found—with serial numbers that matched the ones on the long spring still in Mark Hacking's apartment. The police were pretty sure they knew the exact spot of the killing.

Cops went to the store and talked to Chad and Lesa Downs and the two identified Mark Hacking from the driver's license photo the cops had obtained from Utah driver records.

Mark Hacking rested in the hospital, but he had scant reason to relax.

Helicopter blades chopped the thin air above City Creek Canyon. The sound at the elevation of Salt Lake City, more than a mile high on the ground, is slightly different than it is near coastal regions where the air is more dense at sea level.

The July skies were clear, a welcome relief to the city's residents who suffered through each winter choking on auto exhaust fumes and air pollution combined with fog. The foul Salt Lake City air in winter is a rare blemish on the otherwise pristine skies of Zion. "The Inversion" had been there since the pioneer days, when the skies filled with smoke from wood- and coal-burning stoves. Today, the only difference is that the source is the hundreds of thousands of cars, trucks, and buses that crowd the city's freeways.

The Lori Hacking disappearance was now full-blown, the subject of discussions on news shows on the big three networks, as well as CNN and Court TV. Still more new revelations were about to surface as reporters spoke with friends and family of the couple.

While Lori's mom, Thelma Soares, told the eager reporters about her wonderful son-in-law, co-workers and friends told another story, and it didn't match what she said. They learned that as a youth Mark had been sent home from his Mormon mission.

The revelation of the story that had unraveled Mark Hacking's marriage was destined to unhinge the rest of his life.

City Creek Canyon filled with legions of the merciful, each wanting to lend a hand and find Lori, dead or alive. It was the American way, and even more so, it was the way things are done in Utah along the Wasatch Front. Young and old frequently volunteered to search for hikers lost in the mountains, or skiers missing in the snow, often not to be found until spring melted away the remains of an avalanche.

The people of Zion knew how to search for a missing person, and now these experts filled the canyon, the dome of the state capitol looming above them, wrapped in the scaffolding of a much-needed restoration project.

Hundreds headed from their workplaces to the nearby canyon to join the search as the July sun sank behind the nearby Oquirrh Mountains to the west of the city.

As the searchers jammed the narrow paths of Memory Grove and City Creek Canyon, street reporters barely noticed. They were busy making calls.

Journalists learned at the same time as detectives that Mark Hacking had deceived his wife and family for two years, lying that he was attending classes at the nearby University of Utah campus. The deception was astonishing in its thoroughness. The case of the missing jogger in Memory Grove exploded far beyond a garden-variety missing persons story when North Carolina television station WRAL in Raleigh reported that Mark Hacking hadn't graduated from the University of Utah and had not applied to medical school at the University of North Carolina.

Veteran North Carolina reporter Amanda Lamb went to work ready for another day in the deadline-driven world of local television news. She didn't think it was more than a routine story when the station's news desk assigned her to call the University of North Carolina School of Medicine's media relations department to check out the status of a guy named Mark Hacking.

"I called UNC and asked if he was a student, or had ever applied or had been accepted," she recalls.

The day wore on without a reply to what is usually a very easy question for college administrations to answer to the press.

"The university realized that their role was going to be larger than they had anticipated," she remembers, which was why its media relations department was tardy in getting back to her with an answer.

Finally, late that afternoon, Lamb had her response, and the first huge scoop on the case, a scoop that would have reverberations across 2,153 miles of real estate to a cop shop in Salt Lake City. Lamb was told that Mark Hacking was not enrolled as a student at UNC.

"I called the detectives in Utah and they put me through to a person who was putting things together," she remembers. "I told him what I had found out from UNC and told him that I thought it was important that they know that."

At 5 p.m., Lamb went on live and broke the story.

Unaware of the breaking news, Mark had continued the charade even as he sat in the safe confines of the hospital psychiatric unit, looking his father in the eye and telling him that he had nothing to do with his wife being missing.

Doug Hacking told reporters, "I confronted my son yesterday morning. I looked him in the eye, and I said, 'I need you to tell me if you had anything to do with Lori's disappearance.' I have to tell you that he looked me in the eye and said no."

It wasn't the first time Mark had lied to his father.

He had made a life's work of it. When reporters continued to press Dr. Hacking that morning regarding the rumor that Mark had been found naked in a hotel parking lot the night before, he was almost without words, but managed to say, "I'm sorry that all the attention directed toward our son Mark has hindered our efforts to find Lori."

The response was lame, faltering, and a bit strange, the result of a father whose world had been blown to smithereens by the volcanic eruption of his son's lies.

In retrospect, friends questioned why Lori, universally described as smart enough to knock the top off any test, had been so gullible as to believe her husband for two years.

Why didn't she, a non-smoker, smell the noxious odor of cigarette smoke on his clothes? Had he claimed that his clothes picked up the smell because he was in a room with smokers? Why didn't she smell it on his breath during intimate moments?

Moreover, how did Mark conceal that he wasn't attending classes? He had clearly gone to great lengths to hide the fact that he was dawdling away his time and wasn't even enrolled at the university. Lori would frequently meet Mark on campus for a quick lunch before he had to dash off to class—he'd said—and she had to scamper back to her job at Wells Fargo. Mark also carried around a backpack full of books, seemingly a typical student at the university.

Yet Lori too had been living a lie, presenting the façade of a happy marriage when, in fact, the union was deeply troubled, and had been for a long time.

So was Mark. While he'd presented a happy-go-lucky exterior to the world, he was terribly depressed about the failures that only he knew about. Mark contemplated suicide often. He'd even tried his hand at it, but even failed at that, as he had at so many other things in his life.

Lori had been blinded by the glory of someday becoming a doctor's wife. She was no different from hundreds of young women each year who struggle to make ends meet, even working more than one job, while their husbands are in medical school. For many of them the end result is often heartache when they are unceremoniously dumped after the husband gets the coveted MD.

So it is understandable that Lori Hacking had overlooked Mark's big lie. After all, who wouldn't be blinded by the prospect of a medical practice in the future?

Lori had made a life for herself as Mark claimed to be finishing his undergraduate studies at the university as a late-blooming 29-year-old senior. She maintained old acquaintances and nurtured new ones, such as the two elderly women she had met during her brief sojourn at Block. She also developed church friends such as Christy Goodri, who she enjoyed being around, and whose children she loved. Shortly before her death, the two women took the kids to see *Cheaper by the Dozen*, a blockbuster summer movie, and an appropriate one for Mormon Utah, where large families are the norm.

Chapter Nine

As police combed through the possessions in Mark and Lori Hacking's cluttered apartment on Lincoln Street, they were mindful of an extra burden placed upon them because of a Utah law that had been upheld the previous January in the state's Supreme Court.

Lori was pregnant, they had learned from friends they had questioned and reports in the news media, and as such, under the state's fetal homicide statute, Mark Hacking might spend his final moments on a prison gurney, or facing a Utah firing squad.

Under the Utah law, killing a fetus being carried by a pregnant murder victim was considered a double homicide.

Murder can only be perpetrated upon a person. And under the Utah law, killing both the mother and fetus qualified as a capital offense. The state's Supreme Court left no doubt where it stands regarding the personhood of an unborn.

In their ruling, the court stated, "The common-sense meaning of the term 'unborn child' is a human being at any stage of development in utero, because once fertilization occurs, an unborn child is an 'individual human life' that is 'in existence and developing prior to birth.' "

Critics argued that a fetus does not have the special protection of being a human being, because the state's aggravated murder statute only applies to the murder of a person. Although the author of the bill agreed with the rest of the court that the state's criminal homicide statute covered fetuses at all stages of development, Utah Supreme Court Chief Justice Christine M. Durham argued in a dissent that the fetus was not a person with full constitutional rights.

"Declaring a fetus to be a 'person' entitled to equal protection would require not only overturning *Roe* v. *Wade* but also making abortion, as a matter of constitutional law, illegal in all circumstances, even to save the life of the mother," the justice argued in her dissenting opinion. "In our society, the moral status of the fetus is highly controversial. Our fellow citizens disagree radically over when this period of developing life an egg and sperm combined have matured enough to warrant moral or legal consideration as a person or a full human being."

The Hacking case would keep pro-life activists holding their breath until the body of Lori was found, hoping that an autopsy would produce fetal remains in a state of preservation sufficient to be used in a court of law. If they could get a fetus declared a person who could fall victim to murder, that status might possibly trump all issues and void *Roe* v. *Wade*.

Pro-choice proponents believed that the case had all the makings of a high-profile national platform to enable the opposition's lawyers to take the law all the way to the Supreme Court. Some states have had unborn victim laws on the books for decades and neither state courts nor the U.S. Supreme Court have overturned them. Pro-life advocates appeared to be on firm ground.

The AP reporter hadn't paid much attention to the missing persons story out of City Creek Canyon when it first broke. After all, it was local and would be of only passing interest to the wire service clients who subscribed at radio and television stations and newspapers across Utah, much less the ones on the national wire. But word travels fast among AP clients, and the wire service's Utah office learned that the North Carolina television station had broken a major story on the Hacking disappearance. The AP reporter was now assigned full time to the story as the AP moved the item.

In Salt Lake, a news conference was scheduled with the purpose of updating the media throngs. Now the focus dramatically shifted to the college career of Mark Hacking.

Immediately prior to the news conference, family members were quietly pulled aside and told that there were no records of Mark being enrolled in school.

It didn't take long for matters to get worse for him as journalists dug into his recent past.

The University of Utah quickly confirmed that the would-be medical student hadn't even been in school in Salt Lake since the fall of 2002.

Friends, family, and even slight acquaintances were stunned.

Salt Lake police were astounded by the information coming out of North Carolina. Although they had made the husband of Lori Hacking their prime suspect within minutes of first arriving at the apartment on Lincoln Street, the information coming from the East Coast school was potentially devastating to Mark.

Mark Hacking had now officially and publicly become "a person of interest," a delicate way for the police to call the former University of Utah student a suspect.

Mark's father now faced the media, a strained look on his face.

"The police have been aware of that since yesterday and did not share it with us," he said as he faced scores of cameras. "It still doesn't necessarily answer the question, 'What has happened to Lori?' "

Word had leaked to the Associated Press that Lori Hacking had left her office in tears on Friday of the preceding week after making a call to the University of North Carolina, and when the wire service broke the story, it was open season on the reputation of Mark Hacking.

Friends and family were seemingly stunned that the jokester would lie to such an extent—such a convincing extent. Surely there was some mistake, they said among themselves.

Even Thelma Soares continued to defend her son-in-law in interviews with the media, which now surrounded her every move. She was supported by Mark's parents, brothers, and sisters, and her former husband Eraldo came to Utah from his home in Fullerton, California, to support his ex and stand vigil in the search for his missing daughter. Lori's brother, Paul, came as well, hoping against hope that his sister would be found. A large man, Paul quaked in his grief and anger, incredulous that the brother-in-law who he had come to know so well could have fooled his sister to such an astonishing extent, and not have been caught in the lie.

All of them defended Mark Hacking at first. He was "Mr. Perfect," the ideal brother, son, in-law, husband, and friend.

They didn't know of the demons that haunted him, forcing him to create the persona of Mark the brilliant medical school–bound, walking, talking success story.

Yet they had to have known that there were troubles in the marriage.

Lori had told near-strangers that she and Mark were on the rocks. Yet friends and family circled the wagons around the myth of Mark and Lori's perfect marriage. Their front held even as yellow police tape blocked the doorway of the Hacking apartment.

Television crews now split their vigil between the park near Utah's capitol and the apartment of Mark and Lori Hacking. It didn't take long for the cops to give the media meat grinder more to chew on as the cameras caught officers carrying out potential evidence—paper bags, boxes, and a box spring from what most suspected was the Hacking marriage bed.

Television reporters now had more fuel to add to the rapidly growing fire as they learned that Lori had been almost five weeks pregnant. Speculation immediately began that there was potential for the case to turn into a double homicide.

Meanwhile, Lori's parents again went before the cameras on Wednesday's evening newscasts to plead for their daughter's safe return. They continued to believe that she had been abducted.

Mark's story was unraveling as rapidly. To friends and family, he had been on a fast track to a high-paying medical career based on a good undergraduate education and solid work experience. To the world, the fraud of his deception was exposed when viewers of American newscasts learned that the hulking man with the goatee and bald head was an $8.42-per-hour nightshift hospital orderly, hadn't been enrolled in the Salt Lake university, and wasn't even close to starting medical school in the fall.

The search for Lori Hacking shifted abruptly, if momentarily, from throngs of volunteers crowding City Creek Canyon to hundreds posting handbills with Lori's photograph and a clear message to anyone who might have seen her, no matter how unlikely that was now.

MISSING
FROM CITY CREEK CANYON
OR MEMORY GROVE AREA
LORI HACKING
27 YEARS OLD — 5'4" — 100 LBS
DARK BROWN HAIR   DARK COMPLEXION
PLEASE CONTACT POLICE: 799-3000
WITH ANY INFORMATION

Lori's elderly friends from the Cottonwood office of H&R Block passed out the handbills that had been printed by the thousands on copy machines across the city. Hundreds more volunteers posted them as well, making the young woman's square-framed face, attractive nose, moussed hair, and perfect teeth in a reserved smile as familiar as a box of Betty Crocker cake mix.

As searchers fanned out across the city, the body of Lori Hacking was undergoing a metamorphosis, transforming into a mass of broken bone and tissue crushed in a trash compactor.

The Salt Lake City dump is not meant for the disposal of human remains, yet this was what had happened, because Mark Hacking had tossed the body of his wife aside with the same reverence he would have disposed of an old pair of socks, or the bones of a finished chicken. Now the remains of Lori lay in what he hoped would be her final resting place. There they would compost along with wilted lettuce, carrots not fit for a pot roast, dirty Pampers, and all of the rest of what was unwanted in the life of the city.

The Salt Lake City police quietly dispatched a team to make the long straight run down California Street to sift through the garbage.

After just a few minutes, the smell of the place was overwhelming. They wore shirts and jeans under the cover-alls issued by the city. Some wore baseball caps. Phil Eslinger wore a Boone hat. At the end of the day, the clothes were filthy. Hard-bitten cops who had made a lifetime of smelling the odor of death stripped butt-naked inside their front doors just to escape the residual smell the dump left on their clothes.

The tightness began across his back, then spread to the front of his chest. Inside of him, his lungs burned until he almost shivered from the sensation. The palms of his hands were at once hot and cold, then slightly moist. The walls of the room closed in on him as he sat, then stood, then sat again. Why had he done this to himself? he screamed inside, anger driving his tortured body almost to the brink, then returning to face the agony inside of him again.

His confinement compounded the problem. At work it wasn't as bad. He could concentrate on the patients, or his co-workers. He could entertain them. He was so good at that—entertaining them. That always took his mind off of the problem. Now, locked up and unable to leave even for a breath of fresh mountain air, he thought of little else as the curse of his habit racked his body again and again.

He had enjoyed a full night's sleep, crashing at last into a slumber brought on by stress and fatigue.

But the rest didn't help this problem, because with rest came a body more alert to its own needs, its own cravings.

Mark Hacking craved food. He hadn't eaten much since the night of the murder. But even more than he craved food, he was dying for a cigarette. That would stop the burning inside his lungs. That would dry up the palms of his hands. That would enable his mind to concentrate on more important things such as how to survive the next barrage of questions about his missing wife that were sure to come his way.

Mark needed a cigarette in the worst way imaginable, and he was forbidden to have one.

The cravings came in waves, each a little worse than the one before. He had never felt them so intensely as he did now. Mark cursed himself for allowing the cigarettes to so dominate him. He could create a persona that could trick those closest to him, but he couldn't stop the chemical dependency brought on by the Camels he bought from Paul at the Maverik store around the corner from his apartment.

He had told the clerks at the store never to reveal to his wife that he bought cigarettes from them. Dutifully, they had obeyed his wish. The clerks saw it again and again as they dispensed cigarettes and beer to squeaky-clean "Jack Mormons" a stone's throw from the grave of Brigham Young himself.

The great Mormon pioneer and his followers smoked, drank alcohol, and could curse as well as any sailor hitting the wharves of nineteenth century San Francisco to the west. Even Joseph Smith had operated a tavern in his family's hotel in Nauvoo, Illinois, the prophet's final home before he was murdered by an angry mob.

Brigham Young himself, Utah lore has it, once excoriated the faithful in a sermon within the sacred confines of the Mormon Tabernacle for the disgusting habit of spitting tobacco juice on the building's floor.

No, Mark Hacking's secret smoking habit was safe with the clerks at the Maverik store. It was safe until reporters started nosing around and asking questions.

Meanwhile, confined in his former workplace, Mark couldn't have a cigarette.

Crowds throughout the week swelled and ebbed as the search continued in City Creek Canyon. Estimates of their size vary, but it wasn't uncommon to see between 1,000 and 2,000 searchers looking for Lori in areas in and around the canyon and Memory Grove. By Saturday, many were beginning to give up hope, and most quietly believed that she was no longer among the living.

On Sunday, the crowd of searchers swelled to 3,000. It was the largest turnout in the park since Lori had disappeared. Many searched, while others fanned out to distribute flyers. Two hundred attended a candlelight vigil in Memory Grove as hope faded and family members suffered the despair from the looming possibility that finding Lori was a lost cause.

Meanwhile, Mark Hacking remained hospitalized. Family members told reporters that he was under the care of physicians and would not be released from the psychiatric unit that was now his home until a doctor ordered it.

On Saturday, police brought cadaver dogs to the landfill to join in the search for remains that they were sure were there lying amid the tons of the city's trash.

Trash was on everybody's mind, and a neighbor of the Hackings called police, who found a brown substance at the bottom of his trashcan that the forensic lab described as a protein-rich liquid.

Police also collected a clump of brown hair from a Chevron station at the corner of 2100 South and 300 West. It was sent to the lab as well.

Like all organizations, police departments leak information to friends and trusted journalists. Salt Lake's is no different. Sources within the department confirmed to the *Deseret Morning News* that the cops had seized a bloodstained knife from the Hacking apartment as evidence. It had hair stuck to it as well. The weapon was now part of the growing mountain of evidence against Mark Hacking.

Only a thin veneer of belief remained even to those closest to Mark, a belief driven by love, not logic. His father, Doug, continued to protest his son's innocence, yet his words rang increasingly hollow as Mark sat in the psych ward of the state's largest hospital.

It became increasingly difficult to defend him, no matter how profound the affection his family held for him. The revelations pouring out of North Carolina and Utah were like a hemorrhaging wound. Douglas Hacking knew how to treat such a wound on the body. He was less sure of what to do about his son.

Most powerfully of all, the family was driven by their devout Mormon faith. No matter how much Mark had proclaimed his innocence to others, he had faced those closest to him and told them with a straight face under the ever-present eyes of God that he hadn't killed his wife. Mark would not lie to them, they were sure.

Mark was close to his brothers, and in particular to Scott, who was his trusted soul mate.

"Mark literally wouldn't do anything without talking to Scott," Paul remembers.

The hospital was allowing the prominent medical family to visit their son and brother. The Hackings were of the university, alumni and friends. Lance and Scott Hacking could go see their brother as often as they liked and take as much time with him as they cared to.

Lance and Lori's brother, Paul, met Saturday morning after being told by police that physical evidence had been found and Mark was suspected of foul play. Paul declined to go to the hospital with Lance and Scott to confront Lori's husband. The two brothers went alone.

Lance had made a point of phoning the hospital ahead of time to request that Mark's evening medication be delayed so he would be lucid for their visit. When the brothers arrived that night, Mark appeared coherent, though exhibiting what Lance described as "very real" fear. Mark didn't know what to do, he told them, and both brothers assured him that they would always love him, no matter what. With that, the entire story, held back for so long, came pouring out in explicit detail—the years-long deception about his school enrollment, Lori's discovery of it, and their subsequent argument that night; his brooding over her words during the Nintendo game; his half-hearted attempt at packing, and the discovery of his .22 rifle; the shot to the head as Lori slept; the disposal of the body and the gun.

"Lori's dead, and I killed her," he stated emphatically. Both Lance and Scott thought he appeared to be relieved.

The Southern Baptist axiom "Love the sinner, hate the sin" applied just as well in Mormon Utah as it had in the Old South. Mark Hacking's family now determined to stand by him throughout his, and their, ordeal, no matter what was to happen.

Shortly thereafter, both families announced that further searching for Lori was futile. They said that they had received information from Mark that made the search unnecessary.

The following day, the two brothers went to the Salt Lake police and told them that their brother, the jokester who had entertained friends and family since he was a child, was a cold blooded killer who had dumped his wife's body unceremoniously in a garbage Dumpster.

The family's announcement caused a stir with the media and the public, now certain that a substantial development had come forth to substantiate everybody's supposition that Lori had been murdered, perhaps by her husband. The cops' only comment was that they had received "additional substantive information" from a family member that had to be worked by the department's investigators.

Shortly thereafter, famed Utah criminal defense attorney Gilbert Athay walked through the doors of the psychiatric hospital to consult with his new client.

On Monday, reporters confirmed the appearance of the lawyer. It could mean only one thing. The police were closing in on Mark Hacking and his family members had hired one of Utah's finest and most respected lawyers to run interference with District Attorney David Yocom's office.

One of the rumors then circulating had substantial basis in fact. Lori Hacking's colleagues in the downtown Wells Fargo office were talking, and what they were saying was of profound importance to the police and the case they were building.

Interest in the disappearance was now complete, absorbing, and of true national significance. Producers from all of the network magazine shows were now in Salt Lake speaking with anybody who would talk, and most were more than happy to share what they knew.

Network television producers and guest bookers have a power that print journalists envy. The lure of the camera, the desire to appear on national television, boils under the surface of a surprising number of ordinary citizens. When the opportunity arises to actually speak with someone from one of the shows, those with knowledge of a case sometimes stampede, and it is dangerous ground for a print reporter to stand between them and a television camera.

But three outlets had an edge, and they covered both print and electronic news. The Church-owned *Deseret Morning News* and KSL radio and television often managed to beat the competition, both in print and on the air. The Saints take care of their own in Zion.

Chapter Ten

On Tuesday, July 27, there was movement at the apartment. Police and family members had again converged upon the small complex. Now they watched as cops and family members cleared out the space. At the end of the day, crime-scene tape was removed and the apartments, where residents had been living in a fish bowl, were now able to return to normal. Yet nobody left with a cat. Herbie remained in hiding, traumatized by the loss of Lori and the smell of her blood.

The following day, police took their largest public leap toward confirming that Lori Hacking was the likely victim of foul play when they admitted that they believed it possible that she had never gone jogging in City Creek Canyon or been in Memory Grove at all.

Amateur sleuths now joined the media in believing that Lori Hacking had almost certainly been murdered, and came to the conclusion that Mark Hacking had killed her.

KSL radio's Ben Winslow hadn't been idle, doggedly pursuing lead after lead in hope of breaking another major story. He now reported that the night before she went missing, Mark and Lori had walked into a convenience

store at 900 East and 300 South at 8:30 p.m. The sight-
ing would prove telling, and potentially devastating to
prospects of freedom for Mark. Cameras in the store
had recorded the couple's visit. They would record another visit early the following morning by a lone bald
man who walked up to the counter and asked for a pack
of cigarettes. As Paul, the store's clerk, reached for the
smokes, Mark minutely examined his hands, presum-
ably looking for telltale signs of blood. Nationwide
television would soon broadcast the security video of
the now-debunked would be medical student.

The Salt Lake City police were becoming more
open with the public regarding what they had on the
case. They next revealed that they had confiscated a
Dumpster from behind a ward house at the end of Mark
and Lori's street.

July had turned into August in the blazing Utah sun
as SLPD volunteers combed through tons of garbage at
the city dump. Now there would finally be someone to
charge, they learned through department scuttlebutt.

On August 2, 2004, the department announced that it
had substantive evidence gathered from the Hackings'
apartment, the Dumpster that detectives had seized, and
Lori's car, sufficient to book Mark Hacking on suspi-
cion of aggravated murder.

As the Mormon faithful closed in to protect the Soares
and Hacking families, the media began to report that
Mark and Lori Hacking had both been devout members of the LDS church. The revelation made officials
both proud and wary. Proud that Lori Hacking was
such a perfect Mormon. Wary that Mark, cradled from

birth in the tenets taught by the prophet Joseph Smith and those who followed him, would go so wrong.

And thus far, the media was reporting the marriage was perfect, and most around the couple believed that it actually was.

There is a circle-the-wagons mentality among Utah's Mormons. Justifiably so. Their forefathers had been hounded first out of New York, then Ohio, and then Missouri, and finally Illinois before Brigham Young led them to the perfect land that they called Zion. Today, they remain distrustful of outsiders, particularly outsiders who don't share the faith and aren't Temple worthy.

Salt Lake of late had been besieged by media from outside the state, first with the horde that had descended upon the Wasatch Front for coverage of the Winter Olympics, and then the mobs who'd come to cover the search for Elizabeth Smart.

The Smart case was bad news for the Mormon hierarchy, beyond the obvious tragedy for the young girl and her family. Ever mindful of presenting a squeaky-clean front to a hostile world peopled by disbelievers and skeptics, the Church cringed when the girl was found alive, taken by a street-preaching fundamentalist Mormon who looked like a wild man. Some were actually fearful that the image presented of Elizabeth's kidnapper, Brian David Mitchell, would reflect upon the mainstream LDS Church. To them, his visage evoked memories of Charles Manson. To even call such a man Mormon was anathema, yet reporters continually did so.

The fundamentalists who practiced variations of

old Mormon doctrine were a thorn in the side of the Church. It seemed to many they were put on television all too often. To Salt Lake's modern day LDS members, such weirdos practiced a religion 180 degrees removed from modern Mormonism.

The downtown crowd would be happy if network reporting of Zion only consisted of coverage of the Utah Jazz when they were winning, a concert by the Mormon Tabernacle Choir on PBS, or a skiing competition by *ABC Wide World of Sports*. They were accustomed to presenting the manufactured image of an antiseptically clean mountain paradise. With each day's development in the Hacking case, the image was eroding away.

The establishment didn't like the invasion of satellite trucks, guest bookers, field producers, and reporters who had come to town. Finally, the powers that drive Salt Lake City spoke in the form of an unsigned editorial in the city's secular daily newspaper, *The Salt Lake Tribune*.

"Incessant national media attention no longer serves any purpose," the newspaper wrote.

"Unlike the Elizabeth Smart case, there is no reason to hope that Lori Hacking will be spotted at a truck stop in North Platte, or a trailer park in Yakima, no point in spreading the all points bulletin to everyone with a television set and a cell phone.

So with all due respect and thanks, we have a simple message to the national media paratroops who have parachuted into Salt Lake City for another juicy story on a missing white woman:

Go away."

The newspaper chastised the national media, showing a parochial innocence of the way the news business works that was astonishing.

"This is a local story," it continued, "involving the pain of local people, investigated and prosecuted by local officials and thoroughly covered by the local media. Further reporting of this story for any other reason beyond short updates, is a waste of videotape, ink and, most of all, time."

The writer showed an astonishing ignorance of the importance of such stories to the news hungry national audience.

"When the story is all over it might, in the hands of a perceptive writer, make a good magazine article . . . So it's time for the circus to pack up and leave town. Don't worry. If anything happens, we'll let you know."

The editorial showed how out of touch the hierarchy of *The Salt Lake Tribune* had become in its ignorance of how major media work. Worse, it demonstrated a shallow view fired by a desire of city fathers to manipulate the image of the city.

Members of the national media laughed when they read it and e-mailed it to their home offices, who laughed as well.

Utah's media-savvy residents e-mailed it too, again embarrassed that a place that they loved was being made a laughingstock in the eyes of the outside world.

The fact is simple: The Hacking case would have been interesting in any American city had it happened there. It was made doubly so precisely because it happened in Salt Lake, and because Mark and Lori Hacking were devoted Mormons.

The bottom line: Saints make good copy.

Mark Hacking's confession to his brothers had little effect on their love for him. In the Mormon world, family is everything, even to the point of taking them all, including black sheep, to the Celestial Kingdom to enjoy life in another world where God is man and man can become God. Mark Hacking could still be a part of that world, the family believed. He needed atonement before getting there.

Mark was now among the lowest of the three stages of Mormon glory. He was in the area reserved for murderers, liars, and thieves.

In Mormon theology, there is no such thing as Hell. While the concept of sin is very real, the concept of eternal damnation is alien. There is no forgiveness if the sin involves the Holy Ghost. The theology is much closer to early Christianity than many in the mainstream might expect. The idea of Hell and eternal damnation was amplified when Dante wrote *The Inferno*. Hell, in fact, is a manmade thing that Mark Hacking was unlikely to face for killing his wife, according to a growing number of theologians who are privy to modern biblical scholarship and translation of the gospels.

Yet the family also had a profound belief in law and order, a belief that went to their very foundations as human beings. They knew that for killing Lori, Mark must pay a price, and they further knew that the price the state would extract might be his life.

It was a price that they were reluctant, yet willing, to pay.

Behind closed doors they suffered, now certain that Lori had been murdered by a man they all loved.

The arrest of Mark Hacking came as no surprise to anybody except, perhaps, Mark Hacking. Police simply went into the hospital and took its former employee into custody. They didn't consult prosecutors before taking action.

Mark Hacking was a solid citizen, police learned from searching the scanty records that they had on file. His driving record was unblemished. And he had intervened once when he'd seen a man beating his girlfriend just down the street from his apartment. Moreover, he had told police about a stolen car in his parking lot, and had even reported a strange package in Liberty Park he had discovered while jogging.

Mark's ploy had not worked. He had proved an amateur in the murky world of crime. Again he had failed, not measured up to the standards set by others, even if the others were among society's lowest, the bottom rung on mankind's ladder. Mark Hacking had convinced nobody with his performance in the hotel parking lot when he stripped naked and ranted to the moon and stars shinning down upon Zion. Despite his best effort, nobody believed him, for one reason: The truly insane don't bother to put their shoes back on when they run around naked and rant to any and all who will listen.

The cushy confines of the psychiatric unit were vastly different from the austere surroundings of the

Salt Lake County Jail, which was to become his future long-term residence.

District Attorney David Yocom assigned the case to veteran prosecutor Bob Stott. The question that faced him was simple yet complex: How do you charge somebody with murder when there isn't a body? Of all of the evidence in a murder case, the body of the victim is the most important. It is tangible proof that life had been taken. Until Lori's body was found, the likelihood of convicting Mark Hacking of murder was slim at best, unless he confessed. With Athay in his corner, that prospect was remote.

Furthermore, what murder statute would he fall under? The act of killing his wife didn't subject Mark Hacking to being tried for capital murder unless Stott and his colleagues could somehow bring in Utah's fetal homicide law. That couldn't happen without the body of the deceased, and thus far, the search in Salt Lake City's dump had been futile.

With each passing day, decomposition would make the ability of the state to use that law more remote because of the composting nature of a body lying in the city dump. Mark Hacking was likely to be spared the Utah death penalty no matter how overwhelming the evidence was that he'd killed his wife.

Lawyers come in a variety of sizes, shapes and colors. Some are loud intimidators who can bellow to a jury with eloquence and passion befitting a Southern evangelist; many study these preachers for their ability to move large numbers of people to tears and laughter.

Others work in front of a jury like tiny rodents, gnawing slowly, surely, at a piece of wood until a small hole becomes larger; a lawyer who gnaws at his opponent's case sometimes finds that the hole he finally goes through will reveal victory. Yet others move quietly, lurking in the shadows doing their mischief or good works behind the closed doors of an office or conference room. Some are media-friendly, comfortable in putting spin on the most heinous crime, hoping that a gullible press will re-tell their tall tale with a straight face. Many lawyers come to believe as plausible the often ridiculous explanations they have concocted to find an excuse, any excuse, for the deplorable behavior of their criminal clients. After all, they are paid handsomely to put the best possible face on an otherwise abhorrent act or actor. On occasion, the client is actually innocent.

Money is a lawyer's curse and blessing. The curse is simple: If there is a Hell, surely some of them will find their particular circle to roast on for defending their clients who paid them. The blessing is equally simple: They will live well, eat well, drink well, and have the most articulate friends around until that day comes and they face the Devil himself.

Smart money in Salt Lake City was betting that Mark Hacking, like Brian David Mitchell, the abductor of Elizabeth Smart, would never go to trial. Many had believed that Mitchell was politically too hot for the Church to afford a public airing of Mormon fundamentalism. Predictably, he was sent to Utah's state prison without a trial after a deal was cut between his defense lawyer and the district attorney. Most believed that Mark Hacking had the deck of evidence stacked too high against him for any lawyer to craft a defense that would convince a jury of his innocence.

Moreover, he had chosen a bad state for an insanity defense. Three states don't allow for an insanity defense at all, and Utah was one of them—the others are nearby Montana and Idaho. About half the states would have afforded Mark Hacking a much more hospitable environment for such a defense. They follow the M'Naughten rule, which is based on the British case of Daniel M'Naughten, who had attempted to assassinate the prime minister in 1843. The deranged fellow was acquitted and the defense used by his lawyers is accepted as standard in twenty-six American states.

M'Naughten comes into a trial as an acceptable defense that could result in a verdict of not guilty by reason of insanity if "at the time of committing the act, he was laboring under such a defect of reason from disease of the mind as not to know the nature and quality of the act he was doing, or if he did know it, that he did not know what he was doing was wrong."

Most in the Utah bar and among forensic psychiatrists believed that even if Utah accepted such a defense, it would be impossible to mount in the case of Mark Hacking, who suffered not from insanity, but from a personality disorder.

Gilbert Athay had a client who was clearly bound for the penitentiary. It was just a question of what kind of deal he could cut with Stott on behalf of his client. Stott too was expecting it. He told confidants that the case would never go to trial.

But one thing was certain: Athay would not try

the case in the press. From the beginning, he was circumspect. Speaking with the press or public did not fit into the equation when he represented a client.

Moreover, Athay was in many ways the perfect lawyer for Mark Hacking and a publicity-shy Mormon hierarchy in Salt Lake City: He seldom tries a case and frequently plea-bargains on behalf of his clients. They get the best deal a Utah criminal is likely to receive.

Herbie the cat was still missing. He hadn't been seen since the day of the murder. The last e-mail message that Lori had sent to her mother was a plea to take care of him while she and Mark went to North Carolina. She had planned to drive the cat to Thelma's home in Orem the night of July 21, after work.

When the apartment was empty, Thelma Soares dispatched her friend Debra Gehris and Mark's brother Scott to return to the building to make one last search for the missing pet. The two rummaged through drawers and cupboards, but to no avail. Herbie was nowhere to be found. No amount of calling would bring forth the big yellow cat.

Finally, they caught a glimpse of a hole in the far corner of the closet with wisps of fur around it. They called, but he wouldn't come out.

Now suspecting that Herbie was hiding in the closet, the two went to a local animal shelter and obtained a trap.

The following morning, Herbie was found in the contraption. Thelma had a cat whom Lori had named Izzy. Having lived alone for so long, it was doubtful that Izzy would accept another cat in the house. The Gehrises, however, had just lost Zydra, the cat they had kept for many years, and were happy to take in Herbie. Although he howled mournfully for the first five nights, he eventually adjusted, and now plays and purrs contentedly in his new home.

Robert Stott and Angela F. Micklos of District Attorney David Yocom's office drew the case in the midst of a war with Republican Mayor Nancy Workman whom the DA's office was accusing of misusing county funds and property. The war was bitter and taking its toll on Yocom, who had determined this would be his last fight after a long career of rough-and-tumble politics in the most liberal county in the Beehive State.

Stott, Yocom's able assistant, doesn't remember the initial search for Lori Hacking, but does remember that he became aware of the case of the office's designated hitter for murder prosecutions. It came across his desk in the form of a criminal "information" attached to an arrest warrant for a man already in jail.

They had come so suddenly, so unexpectedly. He was settled into the psych ward of the hospital enjoying the relative comfort and safety of being looked after by healthcare professionals. Suddenly, the cops had appeared and told him they were taking him into custody and charging him with the murder of his wife. His stomach churned, his fists clenched as he was escorted from the hospital in cuffs and placed in the back seat of a waiting police cruiser.

Athay's newest client was driven to the Salt Lake County Jail and immediately found familiar surroundings. The accused murderer sat down in a beige room before a nurse who began asking him questions similar to the ones that had been asked when his brother brought him to the hospital.

Curiously, Hacking gave the police an alias, Jonathan Long. A check of traffic records revealed that several tickets had been issued to someone under that name, and with a similar birthday to Mark, but it couldn't be confirmed that the two were the same person. The alias, and its reason for being, remain a mystery to this day.

When he was arrested, Mark believed what he faced would be just like he had seen on television. Would there be a Detective Andy Sipowitz in his future? Would he be banged around and treated like a lowlife?

He had rushed things when he disposed of Lori's body. He should have taken the time to clean up the apartment from top to bottom, scrubbing like a scullery maid. Instead, he had dumped the gun and thrown away the mattress, but hadn't wiped things up. What an idiot he had been!

Mark now felt anguish for the first time. It wasn't mourning for Lori, but the gut-wrenching feeling that had come to him from realizing that he could spend the rest of his life in jail.

He knew that inmates were given jobs in prison. What mindless task would he be given to do? Would he spend a lifetime stamping out Utah license plates?

Like all young men, he knew that homosexuality and gang rape were an unfortunate reality of prison life. Was that in his future?

Mark was more frightened than he had ever been in

his life on his short ride from the antiseptic confines of the university hospital to the Salt Lake County Jail. After that ordeal, the jail nurse sitting before him was an unexpectedly welcome sight.

The questions were standard triage procedure of admission to a psychiatric unit at any hospital. He hadn't expected them in jail. Now Mark Hacking was again on firm ground, in control and maybe able to avoid life among the rest of Zion's urban inmate population.

The nurse made notations on the forms in front of her. Finally, she said that Mark would shortly see a doctor for further evaluation before being assigned accommodations.

He had passed his first hurdle. He wasn't even booked yet and he was already seeing a doctor. Maybe if he played his cards right and was convincing, he would be taken back to the hospital for treatment.

Suicide.

He had to make them believe that he was likely to commit suicide.

Mark Hacking knew about suicide watch from his work as an orderly at the Neuropsychiatric Institute. It wasn't so bad. Mainly they watched you and took away anything you might harm yourself or others with, including your clothes.

When the doctor came, he was again on familiar ground, easily convincing the physician that he should not be placed in the general inmate population. Mark would be given his own private cell. Convincing the doc had been child's play for him. He knew that the shrink would likely err on the side of caution and place him on suicide watch for a period of observation. Even in jail, physicians practiced cover-your-ass medicine.

He was given a bed and a blanket while he awaited the decision.

Before the trip to his new digs, the staff began the procedures to book Mark into the system, perhaps for a long stay.

They were leisurely about their work, unconcerned that they were now handling Utah's most famous inmate. They had seen it all before, after all, and Mark Hacking was going nowhere else soon.

First his prints were taken, the technician rolling his fingers across a flat surface to secure a clean impression.

Next he was asked to stand, his back to a wall printed with height measurements. The photographer took his picture, a portrait that would forever remain part of the historical record of his visit to the jail.

The entire procedure took eight hours as Mark Hacking was transformed from the privileged son of a prominent physician into a jail inmate accused of murder. Before the new prisoner was finally given his standard-issue jump suit and escorted to a padded cell, he was told that he would be monitored twenty-four hours per day. Mark Hacking had passed the test. He was on suicide watch.

A corrections officer constantly patrolled his eighteen-bed unit, checking on his well-being every fifteen minutes. He would be allowed no visitors while he was on the watch.

Under suicide watch, inmates are classified three

ways, depending upon assessment by professionals regarding the danger they presented to themselves or others: in the most severe cases, the inmate is kept naked except for a rip-resistant blanket; others are allowed a jump suit; less severely afflicted inmates are fully clothed.

The jail carefully protected the information regarding Mark Hacking's level, citing federal privacy laws.

To prevent him from harming himself or others, he was allowed only a bunk, a table, a stool, and a toilet in his cell.

A psychiatrist sees each inmate daily, and only a physician can release an inmate from the unit into the jail's general population.

Mark was now in lockdown. He had a lot to think about and plenty of time to do it. He had none of the familiar things that he had used throughout his life to pass the time. He didn't have a television set to watch. There was no radio. Worse, he didn't have a Nintendo.

Nintendo had caused part of his dropout problem. He had become addicted to the electronic marvel, addicted to matching his skill against the computer to the point that he had dropped out of college. Now even it was gone as he sat in the cell alone, the monotony broken only by the appearance of a guard checking on his welfare at fifteen-minute intervals twenty-four hours a day.

If he hadn't been crazy before, this compassionate form of solitary confinement would surely drive him to that state quickly.

Mark Hacking reviewed his options. He could sit in the cell feigning insanity and be bored to death, or he could risk being included with the rest of the inmates in the giant jail. The gregarious man with the shaved head and goatee decided to get well, and to get well quick.

It was a very different picture of Mark Hacking from the confident, almost cocky, police mug shot of him taken at the jail wearing a blue T-shirt. The picture now flashed across the nation of a man in handcuffs, wearing a flack jacket and dressed in a Salt Lake County khaki-colored jail uniform. Deputies on both sides flanked him as he was led into the courtroom of Judge Denise Lindberg.

The Hacking family had their choice of the blue-bloods of the Utah criminal defense bar, and any of the choices would have been greeted with nods of agreement from other lawyers.

Ron Yengich, who co-founded the Rocky Mountain Defense Fund with Gilbert Athay, is known as an aggressive, in-your-face lawyer given to theatrics. He will get loud to make a point if need be, but beyond the theatrics lies a street fighter with a bleeding heart. He frequently does pro bono work if the cause strikes his fancy. Yengich is the antithesis of the straight-laced Mormon culture that makes up most of his world. He grew up in the shadows of the giant copper mine to the south of the city, the son of a labor organizer. He is acknowledged by most to be the best trial lawyer in town.

In his most famous case, Yengich represented the Mormon document forger and bomber Mark Hoffman against Hacking prosecutor Bob Stott. The representation was successful—the defense lawyer in all likelihood saved the forger's life and secured a plea bargain. Hoffman is currently serving a life sentence in the Utah penitentiary.

In the same firm, Brad Rich is a quiet, thorough litigator whose competence in the courtroom is acknowledged when his peers get together and rate their colleagues.

Bringing up the third leg in this triple-threat firm is Earl Xiax, a laid-back lawyer who quietly and unobtrusively makes magic in the courtroom.

Candice Johnson, the sole female practitioner on the "A" list is known for her innovative approaches in developing a winning game plan, never closing a door on a defense just in case she needs to reach into her considerable bag of tricks if the first plan doesn't work.

Kevin Kerumada exudes quiet competence and is always under consideration when desperate people need to choose the best lawyer available for their money.

Greg Skordas lost a 2004 race for the seat of Utah attorney general, no disgrace for a Democrat in the heavily Republican state. Like the rest, he is a blue chip who is always ranked at or near the top of Salt Lake's defense bar.

But at the pinnacle, the choice almost always narrows to two men, Ron Yengich and Gil Athay. The two so dominate their competition, members of the bar joke among themselves, saying, "If you are innocent, you get Athay. If you are guilty, you run like hell to hire Yengich and hope like hell you get him."

Yet it was Athay, the veteran foe of capital punishment that Doug and Janet Hacking chose to stand beside their son and defend him before the bar of justice.

By all measures, Athay has all of the skills. In the courtroom, he can be as aggressive as a Rocky Mountain grizzly, or as quiet as a mountain lioness stalking an antelope in Big Cottonwood Canyon.

On Tuesday, August 10, 2004, Lori's family came to court to watch the man who had confessed to his brothers that he had killed her. They hoped desperately that he would just plead guilty and get the whole thing over with.

Instead, Hacking stood before the judge in silence. Next to him Gilbert Athay stood as he had with so many defendants before.

Athay told the judge that his client was pleading not guilty.

Lindberg looked down at the defendant from the high bench and asked, "Is that right?"

Hacking nodded, content to let his lawyer do all the talking.

Lindberg scheduled a one-week trial for April of the following year. Mark Hacking would have plenty of time to cool his heels in the Salt Lake County Jail and think about his future.

In seats reserved for the family sat Mark Hacking's mother-in-law, Thelma Soares, the woman who had helped him with his bogus term papers for the nonexistent classes he was supposed to have been enrolled in at the University of Utah.

Afterwards, she spoke outside the courtroom to reporters.

"In pleading not guilty, Mark continues to hurt us," she said. "I feel outrage on behalf of Lori and her baby. Mark heaps insult upon injury."

The grieving mother charged Hacking and his lawyer with "legal posturing," but concluded that that didn't bother her.

Deeply religious, Soares now looked beyond the Utah courts to assess punishment, likely eternity in the Mormon Terrestrial Kingdom, the lowest level of everlasting life among the Mormon faithful.

"I know Mark will one day receive perfect judgment from the only judge who knows every detail of what he did that terrible night."

Chapter Eleven

The families of Mark and Lori Hacking were devastated by the revelations that had been hung out before the nation like a soiled Pamper. They made protestations of ignorance that the couple had had a troubled marriage. They swore before the world that they truly believed that Mark had been a graduating senior at the University of Utah and was medical school–bound.

Some even believed them.

Yet many did not—the chasm of doubt was just too wide to. None would call them liars, though, these family members and close friends of Mark and Lori. Their grief was just too great.

Thelma Soares's grief was profound, evidenced by the anguished look on her face, which was caught by the ever-intrusive television cameras. Eraldo and Paul were more composed, their anguish ripping their guts. They had lost the brightest light of their life, a shining star. Lori had succeeded in everything she had attempted and then some. The estranged but friendly couple could no longer look forward to an old age certain of the love and care of both their son and their daughter. Their grief was unbearable. The two would have to wait until they entered the Mormon Celestial Kingdom to see Lori again.

By September 14, Thelma had recovered her composure enough to appear on the Oprah Winfrey program, telling the TV queen that the family had already bought a headstone for Lori's grave so that a permanent memorial would be in place for friends and family. She sadly acknowledged that the chances of finding her daughter's body were remote.

The grieving woman told Winfrey that she was wearing her daughter's perfume and earrings for the interview. She had previously done the same for an interview with the Church-owned *Deseret Morning News*.

She also wore Lori's ring, telling the talk show hostess that Mark had sold his car to buy it.

Not long before, Thelma Soares established a scholarship fund with the University of Utah School of Business. On the program, Oprah told Lori's mom that she had donated $50,000. Winfrey's donation was by far the largest; however, there were a handful of $10,000 contributions, and some as small as $1. Today, the fund totals more than $180,000. Its first two scholarship recipients would be chosen for the fall 2005 semester.

Douglas and Janet Hacking had experienced an even greater upheaval. Not only had they lost Lori, whom they loved as a daughter, but also they had lost a son who had put the sparkle in many a family gathering. Mark the jokester was gone. Mark the showoff was missing without leave. Mark the do-gooder now sat in the county jail accused of murdering his wife.

The family believed that Mark was insane. On August 6, 2004, Doug Hacking was able to stand before reporters and put a degree of separation between his abhorrence at what had happened, and his understanding as a physician that Mark was suffering from some sort of mental aberration.

"I think it's clear that his whole house of cards he had built, all his deception, had come to an end," Douglas Hacking told a reporter from the AP. "He had been found out. His wife discovered his deception and confronted him with it, and I just think he just saw his whole world collapsing and broke down.

"He just snapped," Dr. Hacking continued. "He did something there's no explanation for. That's the only way I can envision it."

The cops didn't see it that way. They believed that Mark had planned the killing all weekend.

Guilt raised its ugly face in the world of Mark's parents as well. They had reared a confessed murderer who had taken the life of an innocent person as she slept.

Janet Hacking had just seen her son for the first time since his incarceration. He told her he was spending his time "grieving and praying."

But who could believe that? Who could believe anything that Mark Hacking said?

Only a mother would. Perhaps a father might, but nobody else.

Janet and her husband prayed as well, for Lori and

her family. She hoped against hope that people will for-
give us and pray for us. The burden on Mark's parents
was terrible, almost too much to bear for these good and
caring people. As she walked to her waiting car from the
Salt Lake County Jail, the beautiful brunette who was
Mark Hacking's mom carried a weight she had never
dreamed would be upon her shoulders. The sins of the
son had brought guilt upon his mother.

The story had shifted for the press, from accounts of a
not-so-skilled liar, to the pathos and anguish of his
family, and finally to the putrescence of a city dump on
the edge of town.

Reporters had made passing reference to the dump
since early on in the case, knowing that it was the
almost-certain destination of any Dumpster—and a
Dumpster, perhaps more than one, figured prominently
in the case. For most of the previous weeks, the press
had had a much more sexy story to cover. Now they
were faced with a stakeout, and a none-too-pleasant
one at that.

The prospect of searching the dump was daunting.
Annual deposit of garbage in the landfill is 1,068,000
tons.

Mark Hacking was a confessed liar, and many of the
group now detailed to dump duty grumbled that they
didn't even know for sure that he had really deposited
his wife in a garbage container. The police were more
certain—they had secured some evidence from the
Dumpsters he had used to dispose of articles that
might incriminate him.

The day after Lori had gone missing, police called

the dump and told its management they believed that there was some evidence there, perhaps even human remains. They asked that the county please not dump garbage there.

It was a simple matter for them to isolate an area 300 feet in diameter where garbage from the day before had been dumped.

"We build a mountain of garbage," says Jill Fletcher, spokesperson for the Salt Lake City dump. When police called her superiors, they got lucky. Garbage trucks were only two hours into their dump for the day when the call came in. They would be able to search through that trash, then retreat to the mountain created the day before.

Landfill authorities diverted incoming trucks to another area of the vast dump.

Meanwhile, the garbage sat while police devised a dig plan for searching for the body of Lori Hacking. It took a week.

But the cops had volunteers come to the dump almost immediately with cadaver dogs. The animals searched the dump, their sense of smell attuned to Lori's scent, which they had picked up from her belongings seized at the apartment. Yet the search was futile because the heat was too much for the animals.

A week was lost while police devised a plan—a week during which decomposition would take its toll on human remains. With each passing hour, if Lori Hacking was under the tons of compacted garbage, she was composting as rapidly as a discarded head of lettuce. Chances for finding a fetus in her remains became more remote by the hour. So did the prospect of

Mark Hacking being tried for double murder under Utah's fetal homicide law.

Police quickly set up a search zone 300 feet long and 18 feet wide in the vast 550-acre dump.

Each section of the dump was divided into long strips. Each day, a given segment was filled and its location recorded. The depth was a uniform 18 feet throughout the landfill. Authorities knew that if Lori Hacking was in the dump, her body was lying in trash on the north end where the 1,100 trucks that had deposited trash the previous day had finished work. What they would find would almost certainly not be pretty, even if it turned up quickly, because Salt Lake City summer heat advanced decay of bodily tissues. Moreover, after each truck had dumped its load, the pile was compacted by heavy tractor.

On July 19, and during two hours on the 20th, trucks had deposited exactly 4,300 tons of trash at the site. The dump's records were precise.

The Salt Lake police would also have to contend with an 80-degree slope.

Finding bodies in the dump was iffy at best. The department could only boast of a 50 percent success rate, according to spokesman Detective Phil Eslinger, who was often at the scene.

As the landfill's spokesperson, Jill Fletcher was in charge of media relations for her department. She was a rarity. In a profession that traffics in public information, often journalists are fated to deal with what amounts to a public disinformation officer, or worse, one who will impart no information whatsoever. At least with disinformation there is something to work with. A reporter can catch a government official in a lie.

Fletcher is accommodating. She set up the reporters within 50 feet of the Salt Lake City cops' search area.

Then they began their next task. To a person, the press had to become instant experts on police procedures for finding a dead body amidst acres of garbage. They began calling around, contacting law enforcement agencies with experience in the distasteful and smelly job. They quickly learned from the cops that it was worse than almost any task they had ever faced.

"Oh, my God, I don't ever want to do that again," Sheriff Dan Limoges of Union County, South Dakota, exclaimed to his colleagues in Salt Lake City when he was called. He and his men had spent six weeks at a Nebraska landfill searching for the remains of an infant who was alleged to have been put in the dump by his teenage mother.

Zion's cops were calling everywhere there had been a landfill search. They were looking for the voice of experience, a colleague who had been there before who could tell them what to expect, what to look for.

One thing the cops learned was to keep the news media at bay. Fletcher handled the situation for them, keeping the news crews stationed along a road away from the search. The journalists used low-tech tools such as binoculars, and high-tech sophistry such as high-powered lenses on their cameras to zoom in intimately on the searchers.

At night, searchers and reporters both found discomfort because the floodlights were blinding.

Occasionally the cadaver dogs got a break and ran

playfully across the landfill dodging a backhoe as it
lifted garbage. Detectives then started sifting through it.

Tedium quickly became the norm, yet once in a
while the search would stop as cops would walk over to
look in the pit that had been dug. When that happened,
reporters scrambled, knowing only that the cops had
broken the routine and were doing something different.
Maybe that meant they had found something.

The journalists sitting along the road joked among
themselves that they were stationed in a media version
of summer camp, although a smelly one. Some brought
lawn chairs, chips, cookies, and sodas.

Some, like KSL's Ben Winslow, got hooked, wanting
to be on site in case of a find. "The hours drag on. I
know I should go home and sleep," he wrote on the station's blog, "otherwise I'm not going to be on my A
game tomorrow to work. The boss will be mad at me,
but it's so fascinating to see what's going on in the distance. I can't help but watch, and I'll be back tomorrow."

Journalists following the dig quickly learned that a key
ingredient to a successful landfill search is finding material in the garbage that will narrow the search to the
subject's general area, then neighborhood, then block,
and finally their home itself and what the person has
thrown away. At first police were hopeful, acknowledging that, while they had thousands of pounds of trash to
sift through, they had already narrowed the search to
just a few hundred feet of the huge dump, and importantly, one day's garbage.

Yet the stench was overwhelming and getting worse
because of the summer heat. Moreover, unlike Texans,

who can work in 100-degree temperatures, residents of the Beehive State are unaccustomed to working all day long outside and in the bright sunshine of a five thousand foot–plus altitude. Conditions were no better.

Everyone—cops, reporters, Fletcher, all—was becoming too intimate with the workings of a landfill. Night after night, many stayed to see the sun rise as they worked, or watched the crews for signs of the missing woman. Some went home to catch a nap, then were right back at the dump, fearful that they might miss something.

Bored reporters looked for new angles to avoid rehashing the same story day after day, newscast after newscast. One of the first divergent stories was one about potential health hazards to the cops searching for the body of Lori Hacking.

Others found beauty in the landfill, describing the sunsets seen from West Salt Lake City, and the birds that flew to a pond nearby.

Yet at sunset, the mosquitoes came out, pesky critters that seemed larger than garden-variety pests. One wag described them as being the size of small cars. Others joked that the mosquitoes had mutated after exposure to large doses of methane and other chemicals dumped there.

A news photographer even went so far as to wear ski pants to the dump daily to try to prevent bites to his legs, claiming that the landfill's mosquitoes could bite through normal jeans.

For Mark, the general population areas of the jail were almost as bad as the psych lockup, where it was at least relatively quiet. In general, it was noise all the time, 24/7. And Mark quickly found that the men he was now around were far different from the college-educated people he had known all his life.

Jail is like the rest of civilization, just a little less civilized. It is inhabited by the fat, the thin, the sick, the well, the handsome, and the ugly. Mark had never been around poor people. Now they were his neighbors and he learned that the poor speak a different dialect from the privileged Mormons with large happy families he had grown up with.

And yes, there were Mormons there as well. Church-going Mormons at that, and each and every one of them had a story. Some were willing to tell it, others weren't.

But most of all it was the noise that could drive a person crazy in this man's world where it was smart to appear tough, and not so smart to appear sensitive.

Mark's size, his shaved head, and his goatee would serve him well during his first days in the general population of the Salt Lake County Jail.

At least he didn't look like one of the sensitive ones.

Detective Phil Eslinger kept his back to the wind. They all did as they sifted through the city's trash.

Dump duty wasn't part of his job description, but he did it anyway with about twenty other cops.

On the first day, the cops placed a team in the field hoping for a quick hit. Initially, it was just a visual search, walking around the landfill looking at the surface as the cadaver dogs did their work. By the second day, the police learned that some of their colleagues were not physically or emotionally equipped for dump duty. In fact, some were throwing up, their stomachs in involuntary revolt at the decay they were seeing and smelling.

"It was just more than they could handle," Eslinger remembers.

The cops quickly learned that the compacted garbage, even after only a day, was difficult to pry loose and they ordered in a front-end loader, a tractor with a big scoop on one end attached to powerful hydraulic lifts. The machine was capable of moving tons of trash in a relatively short period of time.

The machine lowered its scoop, then its large rubber wheels dug into the surface as the tractor struggled, its engine belching black smoke. It broke the surface of the compacted debris, digging in until the scoop was filled to capacity. It then raised the container high in the air as the operator moved toward the tipping face, a spot designated under normal circumstances for the trucks to dislodge their loads.

Now the face was designated as a deposit area where the cops could go through the refuse carefully and methodically, looking for the slightest clue that they were finding trash from Lori Hacking's neighborhood.

"It made a huge pile," Eslinger remembers. "Soon we had it broken into sections and spread as thinly as possible."

The Salt Lake cops quickly developed a game plan. Each area they would search would be limited to 100 tons.

In a state obsessed with symbols—the beehive, the Angel Moroni, the spires of the Temple itself—perhaps none is more enduring than the gull. Legend has it that in 1848, shortly after the arrival of the Mormon pioneers, the Salt Lake Valley was plagued by a swarm of locusts that threatened the precious crops that had been planted to get the settlers through the cold Utah winter. At the eleventh hour, just as all of the crops were about to be destroyed, the Mormons prayed for a miracle. It came in the form of flocks of seagulls that swooped in and ate the locusts.

A monument in Temple Square celebrates what is called in Mormon lore "the Miracle of the Seagulls." While there is little evidence in contemporary accounts to support the legend, it is retold each year and passed along from generation to generation among the brethren.

Yet it could easily have happened, because gulls do inhabit the shore of the Great Salt Lake and are frequently seen flying over the city itself and picking edible garbage clean, even at landfills.

Salt Lake City's dump, while not directly on the giant lake, is close enough to it to attract seagulls that are quick, resourceful, and hungry enough to grab a bite before the compactors roll over the garbage and render it hard as a rock. So when a front-end loader arrived to churn up the recently buried garbage, the ever-vigilant seagulls flew into the dump in droves, quickly making a nuisance of themselves.

But the seagulls were only a minor inconvenience compared to a more pressing annoyance, the ever-present dust from desert sand churned up by the heavy equipment working the dump.

In fact, the dust eclipsed the presence of flies, a constant in any landfill.

"The dust was just horrible," Eslinger remembers. "It was so bad, I don't think the insects even wanted to be there."

The officers stood four abreast and shoulder to shoulder holding bent implements similar to hay forks, but with pointed tines, their backs to the desert wind and dust as they looked for evidence and the remains of Lori Hacking.

The motion the searchers used was mindless, repetitive. They stood bent over as they worked, wishing that the garden tools would turn up the long-sought evidence from the compressed garbage they were walking on. Occasionally, the sharp points of their implements would burst a bag, and its rotting contents would spill upon the surface. That's when the flies attacked, quickly followed by the aggressive gulls.

On the first day the searchers were issued fire boots with steel shanks. Their first duty had been to attend a lecture on the health hazards they would encounter during the search. Most of those hazards could come from the indiscriminate dumping of hospital waste. Others would come from hazardous materials such as chemicals.

After that it was the tetanus shots, required of any cop working the down-and-dirty search site.

For ten hours each day, the cops did this, determined to find the body of Lori Hacking—hoping her husband hadn't told another lie and dumped her somewhere else. The teams of twenty men and women worked four days, then were off for a day, then returned for four more days in the dump. There were sixty cops out there, sixty sick and tired cops.

Chapter Twelve

Catching a whiff of the dump, Detective Phil Eslinger, 42, dabbed Vicks on his finger and put it up his nose for the umpteenth time. The veteran cop had learned that the pungent odor of the petroleum jelly–based cold remedy cut the sickening smell of the dump fairly well, at least for a while. Eventually he would have to open the jar and repeat the routine.

The detective had grown up in Albuquerque and lived all over the West until he arrived in Utah with his parents. His dad was a financial printer, the most exacting job in a broad field. As Phil grew up, he worked odd jobs to support an amateur football habit. This team traveled around, playing exhibition games. Eslinger once got cold-cocked in Austin, Texas, and ended up in a hospital emergency room.

But being a cop suited the soft-spoken, articulate man. The work was interesting, and you could do a little good in the world.

He looked down as he raked some more debris. How many thousands of times had he put the rake forward, drawn it back to reveal a thin layer of trash, then pulled it behind him to begin the process all over again?

Something dull and straight caught his eye. He poked, and it was hard. Quietly, without alerting the others on either side of him, he bent down and picked up what he thought was a bone. Disappointed, he quickly threw the stick back to what passed for ground below his feet. It was another false alarm. How many had there been? Eslinger wasn't keeping count.

He had watched the cops come, and watched some of them go. He didn't judge the ones who left the dump duty to guys like him. Some folks just didn't have the stomach for this kind of work.

Eslinger liked to think of himself as task-oriented, focusing on the job at hand.

He stopped again, this time reaching into his pocket for a plastic vial of eye drops. Like the jar of Vicks, the wash was an essential tool of dump duty in the desert, where no matter how hard a man tried, the blowing sand constantly got into the eyes.

Eslinger was alert to specific items, things that would tell them they were perhaps getting close to the load containing Lori Hacking. He, and all of the cops serving on the task force, kept a special eye out for mail. An address could be a key indicator of exactly what neighborhood or building's trash they were working.

"If we could get a letter with their address on it, that would mean that we were getting close to the body," he recalls. The cops believed that Lori had been dumped at the hospital, but still weren't certain, because Mark hadn't told his brothers where he had disposed of her. "I also looked for dates," he says. The closer the date was to the date of the alleged murder, the better.

Archeologists' favorite sites to dig are dumps and

latrines. It is these unsavory places that the artifacts of everyday life are found in abundance.

An archeologist wouldn't have been surprised, but Eslinger was when the team found several wedding rings, the sad remnants of happier days in the lives of some Salt Lake residents. Eventually the ring count would total more than sixty pieces. It was a sad thought, sixty marriages, sixty memories, sixty weddings cast aside in a swath of garbage 18 feet wide and 300 feet long.

Eslinger thought of things like this as he continued the repetitive movement with the garden tool, raking the trash toward him and looking down. Then one day his pulse quickened, a cop's response to a possible break.

The first day had been so exciting, he remembered. In front of him had been a blood-soaked pillow. But the excitement quickly turned to disappointment. The pillow was from the surgical suite of a hospital. It was medical waste. After finding the fiftieth similar pillow, Eslinger and his fellow searchers simply swept them behind.

But it wasn't medical waste when the searchers' probe struck a body. It was in an advanced stage of decomposition. He looked down to see very little flesh and connective tissue. The bones were intact.

It was a pig.

Duchesne County Chief Deputy Wally Hendricks knew the call would come. Early on, he and his crack team of cadaver dogs had searched briefly at the site in the punishing summer heat. Hendricks' team was known throughout the Western states as the best, smartest, most skilled, and agile search dogs in the business. They had found bodies in Nevada, Idaho, Wyoming, New Mexico, Colorado, and of course, Utah.

Wally, with team members Mona Jean McGinnis and Cheryl "Bunny" Young, were up on the Green River conducting a search with other members of the team when the call came from Detective Cordon Park of the Salt Lake City Police Department to the chief's cell phone. The team was needed. They would have to leave the tiny piece of desert and mountain paradise that they called home.

Picturesque Duchesne sits at the base of the majestic Uinta Mountains, Utah's tallest. It was the site of Fort Duchesne, established in 1886, built to guard the Indian frontier of eastern Utah, western Colorado, and southwestern Wyoming. It is an unlikely place for a crack team of detectives specializing in finding decomposed bodies to be located.

Yet there is logic to the group's formation, after all. The High Uintas soar to more than 12,000 feet. They are some of the tallest mountains in the West. They are also a wilderness, snowed in each year until spring, and largely devoid of human population.

In short, people get lost among these forbidding peaks. They die, and often are not found quickly by search teams sent to recover them. Not all bodies in the Rocky Mountain region are homicides.

Hendricks's team had been formed nine years before, largely to find the unfortunate victims of avalanche, skiing accidents, misdirection, and just plain stupidity in the great outdoors. The fact that their training dovetailed with homicide investigations was a happy coincidence.

The members have strange names for investigators whose specialty is finding death: Missy, Tubby (a neutered male), and Kerri, all Border collies; Minnie, a chocolate Lab; and Sage, a black-and-brown German shepherd. They are the famed cadaver dogs of Duchesne County. They are known across the mountain region and into the vast deserts of America as the Uinta Mountain Search Dogs.

Their training in finding death is as complete as the training a dog goes through to compete in Madison Square Garden.

"We will get the soil or bedding next to the body that the entire decomposition process has gone through," he explains. "We imprint them on that. Eventually they give a desired response, either sit, or lay down, when they smell that for a reward."

Hendricks says that there are two degrees of training the dogs achieve, general cadaver dogs, who can simply give a basic response to human decay, and forensic cadaver dogs, animals that can respond at the microscopic level to things such as cleaned-up bloodstains.

In their six years as forensic cadaver dogs, Missy, Tubby, Kerri, Minnie and Sage worked some famous cases, finding victims such as Tricia Ann Autry, a woman found in Utah's Cache County at a coyote research farm. She was alleged to have been killed by Cody Lynn Nielsen, a defendant in Logan.

"The dogs hit on half her jawbone," recalls team member Mona Jean McGinnis, an administrative worker for the sheriff's department. "He had also burned her and spread remains in another area."

She remembered other cases that the team went out of the area to work for other agencies, such as a woman they found on the White River.

"Minnie found her," McGinnis says fondly.

During a search in Idaho they identified and flagged an Indian's bone. The remains had been dead for more than 100 years. At home in Duchesne, some local folks were moving some rock around when they came upon something strange, an old shoe. The dogs found its owner, buried 112 years before.

In a New Mexico village, the dogs found evidence, but not a body, in a homicide case, and in Juab County, Utah, they found a skull.

When Hendricks and his team made the 118 miles across the Wasatch Mountains to Salt Lake City, the group headed directly toward the Hacking apartment so that the dogs could get a whiff of the odor of Lori Hacking, still lingering in the place. They then went to two other locations, carefully keeping where they had worked secret from the press and public. The team would work on and off looking for the body for twenty-seven days.

The buzz in Utah's legal circles concerned what Gil Athay would do with his newest and most prominent case. Smart money was betting, if it bet at all in this straight-laced enclave, that the case would never go to trial. If there was ever a case in which the state had the defendant hog-tied for butcher, it was *State of Utah* v. *Mark Douglas Hacking*.

Of course, strange things happen. In Galveston, Texas, a jury was swayed by two of the Lone Star

State's finest attorneys, Dick DeGuerin and Mike Ramsey, to acquit billionaire Robert Durst of murder for killing, and then butchering, the body of his neighbor and throwing his pieces into Galveston Bay.

But Utah lawyers knew that Bob Stott had skills far beyond those of the Texas district attorney. His competence had been proven by decades of successful prosecutions. It wasn't likely that he would lose such a slam-dunk case as the killing of Lori Hacking.

No, smart money was betting on a plea bargain before Christmas.

The art of the plea is delicate, pitting two highly charged egos, the prosecutor and the defense attorney, in a game in which the stakes are a client's life. The result of the standoff is measured in terms of years of incarceration. In the overwhelming majority of cases, the prosecutor holds almost all of the cards.

While the defendant sits in an often cold, dank, noisy jail, sweating, his lawyer sometimes has a cavalier attitude. Virtually all sincerely want to get the best deal possible for the person who is paying them, but the lawyer, unlike his employer, is able to go home to a soft bed in a quiet room, have a quiet drink, and drift off to sleep. The defendant, all the while, often goes sleepless with worry, concerned that his lawyer cares less about his case than he does.

A large portion of clients expect the impossible, making a reasonable plea negotiation difficult for a lawyer. A client such as Mark Hacking, suffering from narcissistic personality disorder, can make an attorney's job almost impossible. Such defendants crave the spotlight, and the spotlight of a sensational murder shines very bright indeed. In these cases, the defendant is on stage, playing to the biggest audience of his life. A plea of guilty would end all that. The defendant would quickly fade into the obscurity of the inmate population of a state prison.

Gil Athay could have his hands full.

City government runs on the paper generated between departments as funds are transferred within its precincts. Such was the case in the search for Lori Hacking. As searchers dug through trash, computers at Salt Lake's City and County Building whirred as bean-counters tallied up the tab for finding the body of the murdered Wells Fargo employee.

The Salt Lake City cops were being charged between $20 and $50 per hour for the services of the dump's workers, and heavy equipment such as the front-end loader being used in the search, and a bulldozer and excavator.

Some, like the Duchesne cops, their volunteers, and dogs didn't charge the city anything more than for food and lodging. Their pay, such as it was, came from a state fund set up to reimburse cities for man-hours spent on search duty. In some cases, Hendricks's team members even paid for their own meals, not charging Salt Lake anything. All told, they would log 2,000 man-hours and 712 dog-hours in their search, billing the state fund a paltry $2,158 for their time logged in twenty-seven searches.

The animals are trained in their grisly work using whole cadavers, not just body parts hidden in the woods. Hendricks also brings rookie dogs to homicide or accident scenes where the dogs smell the body in the place where it decomposed, not in the clinical atmosphere of an institutional setting such as an autopsy room. The training of the cadaver dogs is ongoing, placing them in as many conceivable situations as possible where death might have occurred.

Hendricks determined that his team would stay at the Salt Lake dumpsite for three to four days each time they came to the city.

"You want to maximize your dog's potential," he says. He quickly decided to work the four-legged cops at night for a variety of reasons.

"The landfill generates heat," he said of the giant compost pile. "In the daytime, the temps were in the eighties and nineties, but the surface would be one hundred and four."

Such conditions were not favorable to the dog team being able to concentrate on the task at hand, following their noses. For the animals, working in the daytime was like walking barefoot on asphalt in July. The dogs would be concentrating on the discomfort in their feet rather than catching the scent of a decomposing body.

Moreover, there was another distraction to working a summer day in the dump.

"There were ten million seagulls there in the daylight hours," he remembered. And the insects and gulls went away at night.

"What's more, we didn't interrupt the daytime operations of the landfill with the search," he said.

Not everybody was sold on taking the Uinta team into the landfill, Hendricks remembers. The thinking was that there would be just too many odors of rotting organic matter in the dump for the animals to concentrate on finding just one scent.

Wrong.

"The dogs were hundred percent effective," he says. "Our dogs moved four thousand five hundred tons of garbage."

The dogs frequently found medical waste in the dumpsite.

"That just kept us encouraged," Hendricks says proudly. "That meant the dogs were working."

The dogs worked nose to the ground after their handlers released them from any restraints to roam free. When they believed that they had caught a scent, they went into a sitting position, telling their human team members that something was up.

"They are so intent in what they are doing when they are on the scent," McGinnis says.

In fact, the dogs flagged the spot where Lori's remains were ultimately found.

Hendricks wasn't surprised by the Uinta dogs' accuracy. "The dogs made alerts, but the people just hadn't dug there yet."

The hiring of Gilbert Athay to defend Mark Hacking wasn't greeted happily by some faithful, who believed that the man now in the Salt Lake County Jail should show remorse. They were critical of Doug and Janet standing by their son with both emotional support and their money.

Immediately after Mark's confession to his brothers had become public, the family stood before television cameras acknowledging that their son and brother would have to pay the price for killing his wife, even if it meant losing his own life in an execution. Yet they had hired Athay, a blue-chip lawyer in any Utahan's book, to defend him. Athay's skills didn't come cheap.

A Bountiful woman, Shirley Greenhalgh, summed up the feelings of many in a two-paragraph letter to the Church-owned *Deseret Morning News*:

> I am appalled that Doug and Janet Hacking are paying high-priced attorney Gil Athay to defend their son. Mark has confessed to killing his wife; they know he is guilty. Giving financial aid for their son's defense sends a message that they support his actions. It is also adding insult to injury for the Soares family.
>
> Remorse and restoration are part of repentance; I see no remorse on Mark's stone face. As a mother, I can appreciate the Hackings' desire to protect their child, but who was there to protect the Soares' child? Let Mark pay the price for his senseless choice.

The loss of a child weighs heavily upon a parent. To not find their body, to think of a loved one lying rotting in a city dump, is too much for anybody to bear.

While the two families had been close, appearing together before the press, and reportedly going to each other's houses after the disappearance of Lori and the announcement of her murder, there was a strain. The strain became a crack, and then a rupture for at least one of the parents.

Eraldo Soares couldn't contain his anger at the man who had murdered his little "Angel Baby."

Thelma could continue to be consoled by the Hackings. Eraldo wouldn't be. Mark Hacking had murdered his little girl. He had lied to her and the rest of the family and gotten away with it to the point that everybody had believed that he was going to be a doctor someday. When Lori had caught him in the lie, Mark had been a coward, and rather than admit the truth and face the wrath of his wife, he had skulked into their bedroom, pointed a rifle at her head, and pulled the trigger, snuffing out the brightest light in the lives of her parents. Mark, in Eraldo's eyes, was the worst kind of coward.

Chapter Thirteen

Gil Athay stays in good shape, say his friends. Now in his 60s, the stalwart of the Salt Lake bar takes advantage of the outdoor amenities right at the nearby ski resorts in areas such as Brighton, Snowbird, and Sundance, and the liberal stronghold of Park City. In his pocket, the lawyer has his season lift ticket at the ready, just in case he can snatch a moment on the slopes.

Athay is fit, both physically and mentally. In court before a hearing, he is animated, constantly moving. He chats with clients and their families, he chats with deputies, he chats with court officials. Athay is a study in motion, a balding smallish man whose looks belie his age. He could easily pass for ten years younger.

When he takes a case to trial, "he approaches cases from a very analytical standpoint," his friend, federal prosecutor McCelvy says. "He has an excellent ability to examine the strengths and weaknesses of a case and tailor his defense on them.

"He's not as flamboyant as Yengich. He is analytical."

If he goes to trial, McCelvy says, Athay doesn't waste time challenging issues that will make his client look bad. If, for example, his client has hit someone

with his car and then run away, he'll stipulate that before the jury, acknowledging the worst, "and then he'll
move on to focus on the issues he'll challenge successfully.

"He's an intellectual."

He'll then endear himself to the jury, telling self-
deprecating stories that might prove embarrassing to
him. The twelve men and women before him quickly
like the consummate gentleman with the great sense of
humor. He's not the first lawyer to use such tactics, but
he's definitely one of the best at using them, friends,
associates, and judges say.

If, in the unlikely event Athay ever took Mark Hacking's case to trial, he would be a formidable opponent
to Bob Stott.

Mark Hacking sat in the cell of the Salt Lake County
Jail and thought about immortality. Earlier in his life,
the "devout" Mormon had given little thought to the
actual theology of his faith. Few young Mormons did,
actually. They certainly didn't go into the founding
tenets of the religion established by Joseph Smith. Few
knew, for example, that the church founded by the
prophet was cut from the same mold that made commu-
nism, predating the theories of Karl Marx. The prophet
urged his followers to give their wealth to the Church to
share. Many did, much to their chagrin.

Remnants of the share-the-wealth philosophy of
early Mormons remain to this day. In early 2005,
Utah authorities attempted to break up a land trust es-
timated at $100 million, owned by the polygamous
Fundamentalist Church of Jesus Christ of Latter-day
Saints (FLDS). The sect broke off from mainstream

Mormonism when Utah abolished the habit of plural marriage.

Members of the FLDS created the trust in 1940. They had turned over their property to the church, much as followers of the original prophet, Joseph Smith, had asked Church members to do in the early days of the church. The idea was that all could share in the community's assets. Members could build homes on trust property, but were viewed by the church hierarchy as tenants. It all worked until dissident members were excommunicated by church leaders and wanted their piece of their equity.

Much of their history has been hidden by an authoritarian hierarchy, since Brigham Young took over at the prophet's death. A great deal of history, critics charge, has been swept under the rug to obscure what the early Mormans believed.

Mark was a Mormon of convenience, not fact. He was a smoker, probably a drinker, and he violated the other rules of Joseph Smith's Word of Wisdom.

The façade Mark had presented as a moral man in good standing with his Church was now shattered. The falsehood of his life was now transparent. No amount of jailhouse piety would slip past a Mormon judge in Utah, wise to the ways of the state's criminals. There would be little sympathy for him.

There was absolutely no sympathy from the Mormon who would prosecute him. Bob Stott, described as one of the most devout members of the sect in Utah, is not fanatic about his religion and keeps it to himself. He is devout, tolerant of other religions, and, in a sect which calls itself the one true Church, doesn't confine his list of close friends and acquaintances to the people he surrounds himself with at his ward house.

As a devout Mormon, it was only natural that Stott would act in the best interests of the Church. Yet he was an equally devout lawman.

Now, the Hacking case had been thrust into his lap and cynics charged the defendant would never go to court because the Church was so averse to high-profile cases drawing national media attention.

Stott never believed that the case would go to trial, but not for that reason. From the beginning, he had been open to a plea by Mark Hacking. But first he had some thinking to do.

"Negotiating a murder case is generally a little different than other cases," he says. "Generally, I will approach the defense first, but not always. First, I have to determine for myself, after careful analysis of the case, what a fair and just resolution, for the victim and society, would be."

After Stott came to the conclusion that the case, or any case for that matter, was worthy of a plea bargain, he then had to get Yocom to sign off on the deal. That was never difficult. Yocom so trusts Stott that approval is virtually always assured.

His next step was to inform the victim's family. Like others in most states, Utah prosecutors don't have to get their consent to the plea, they just need to let them know that a deal is in the works.

Stott describes his mode of dealing with a defense attorney as casual after he opens the door to a plea.

"I make one offer, and the defense attorney knows

that my first offer is the only offer unless something comes up out of the blue," he says. "Then our discussions are usually cordial. The defense attorney will try to point out reasons why I should make a better offer or accede to his offer."

Ever cordial, Stott patiently plays along.

"I listen politely, banter with the defense attorney, and remain firm on my original offer."

Stott finds it unproductive to argue or become strident in the negotiations.

"Seldom does rancor or bitterness arise, except sometimes in capital cases where the stakes and passions are higher."

The pull and tug can be endless, going on casually, but seriously, sometimes until just before trial.

Stott has fun with it for the most part, but not always.

"With some defense attorneys, the process of plea negotiations is almost entertaining and spirited; with some, it is perfunctory and dull."

Stott and Athay both know the likely outcome as soon as plea negotiations begin.

Everything has value to a lawyer. For civil litigations, the value of a case is calculated in terms of awards and legal fees. For criminal lawyers, the worth of a case is determined in the amount of money an attorney can receive for representing his client, and the amount of punishment assessed or agreed upon. The Hacking case was no different, and both Athay and Stott knew its value.

"With a seasoned veteran like Gilbert, we come to the table knowing that both of us know what the case is worth and the probable outcome. Beating around the

bush is not necessary, and usually little is done to per-
suade the other one differently, since we respect each
other's situation and analysis. The facts and the desire
of the victim play heavy in these cases. I know that, the
experienced defense attorney knows that, and we know
each other know that."

In the case of *State of Utah* v. *Mark Douglas Hacking*, the only ones for whom the outcome remained a
mystery were the public. The deal between the two seasoned lawyers was as solid as the Prophet's revelations. The defendant's future, though, was as flimsy as
Utah snow just before an avalanche.

Bob Stott was so certain of the outcome that he
didn't prepare a case at all. In a lunch with Athay in a
greasy spoon across the street from his office, Athay as
much as told him he wouldn't mount a defense of
Mark Hacking. Stott's trust for his fellow lawyer was
so strong that he just sat back and did nothing, secure
in the knowledge that the defendant would ultimately
face a judge and be sentenced to a long term in prison.
The deal of the plea bargain was cut from the very earliest days of Mark Hacking's confinement. He knew
the case would never go to trial as early as a week after
Mark Hacking had been charged.

Yet Athay did craft a window-dressing defense. It
was highly unlikely it would ever be used, but it
sounded better than nothing when he was pressed by
the media regarding what kind of case he was eventually going to present in court.

He learned early on that his client had been injured
when he'd fallen and banged his head while doing some
roofing work. Athay, like any good criminal defense

attorney, jumped on the fact that Mark could have suffered a neurological as well as physical injury from the bang on the noggin.

Athay claimed that he was in contact with an expert on such injuries, who would argue that they had provoked uncharacteristic behavior resulting in homicide.

Stott knew that his opponent wasn't working on a defense at all, any more than he, Stott, was working on a case to be prosecuted. This would be a plea, pure, simple, and as sure as Utah honeybees love the mountain flowers.

And yet Athay persisted in telling press and public that brain trauma had changed the personality of his client. It was all that he had to go on, and he would milk the theory for everything it was worth until the prison door closed behind Mark Hacking.

Chapter Fourteen

Friday, October 1, started as usual for Sergeant J. R. Nelson. He arose at 6 a.m., as was his habit, dressed, and headed to work.

For a man with more than two decades on the force, Nelson looks in many ways like an open-faced Irish kid. He still retains the carrot-top red hair of childhood, but now there is a red mustache to match. The face is flushed, and the eyes are blue.

The veteran cop had come to Salt Lake City from his home in Flint, Michigan. The Northern accent still hangs on his tongue like the chill of the fog off Lake Huron. Nelson had followed friends to Zion to get away from the bitter winter he had grown up with.

As the administrative sergeant of the city's 120-cop Pioneer Patrol Division, it was Nelson's duty to oversee moonlighting cops collecting change from parking meters downtown. It wasn't chump change he was dealing with here. One parking meter in a busy section of any American city can generate as much as $20,000 in the course of a year—enough coins to make it necessary that a senior cop watch over the collections for no better reason than to keep honest men, well, honest.

Like much else in police work, the job had become routine. He would soon transfer to the Detective Division.

In Salt Lake, the weather was much more mild, and the sun shone mostly, except when the winter inversion covered the valley in clouds. He had assimilated well, and now the city at the foot of the Wasatch Range was home.

Nelson arrived at work at 7 a.m. ready to assume the routine duties, bone up on what had gone on in the city overnight, and then begin his day. Then it dawned on him that he was in the wrong place. He was supposed to be at the dump.

The confession of Mark Hacking had the tongues of the faithful wagging along the Wasatch Front, the communities along I-15 that butt up against Utah's most famous mountains. Mormon men spoke quietly among themselves about how Mark Hacking's wife must have provoked him.

Perhaps indicative of this was Bryan, a cabbie who drove this author to the Salt Lake City Airport several months later. He summed it up as he related a conversation with his father as a Book of Mormon lay on the seat.

"My father agrees with me that she challenged him," he said as he explained the male dominance inherent in Mormon households.

The Yellow Cab driver is a self-admitted Jack Mormon. Backsliding Saints who love to gamble, smoke, and drink are derisively called "Jack Mormons." To many of them, the term is a badge of pride at having escaped the strict rules of Mormon orthodoxy. My cabbie had once participated in a successful mission to Australia.

"What do you think of the Prophet?" I asked, trying to get insight into a religion in which one man is venerated as one who speaks with God. I was speaking of Joseph Smith.

"I would die for him," he says, despite his current lapsed status. "I would die for Hinckley. He is a good man. I would die for the Church."

He explained that Mormon men will be lords of their Celestial Kingdom. Many believe that the kingdom begins right here on earth, even in a small apartment on Lincoln Street.

Yet Bryan is appalled at the shooting of Lori, because killing is an abomination by his standards.

"He will be excommunicated," he said. "He almost surely already has been."

Sergeant Phil Eslinger and the men searching the dump received a request from one of the Salt Lake City police captains that the father of Lori Hacking wanted to speak to the cops on the scene.

"I have come to realize that you aren't going to find the body intact," Soares told them as they interrupted their digging. "Keep up your work, even if you find the smallest remains, so that she can be buried."

Eslinger, like the other searchers, was hit hard by the sincerity and anguish of the father's speech.

"He was emotional, and his speech was heartfelt," the veteran cop remembers. "He came before us and talked to us out there . . .

"We desperately wanted to give the family a sense of closure," he says. "If some of my family members were in the same situation, I hoped that somebody would be able to do the same for them."

Stott and the detectives were in a quandary. They had a murder charge without a murder weapon, a killing without a body, and were working with scant physical evidence. Only specks of blood had been found at the crime scene, and in Stott's opinion, the blood evidence was in such short supply, he questioned whether the lab results would stand up in court.

At Salt Lake City police headquarters, a 1960s building undistinguished by its architecture, detectives attempted to bolster their case. They were unaware that Stott and Athay had already cemented their deal.

J. R. Nelson arrived at the dump, donned his protective gear and found that a cop named Jason Simpson didn't have a partner that day. The teams were accustomed to working in pairs, and he joined the man as the two began to pull their hay rakes in the repetitive motion now painfully familiar.

Morale was low. The police had spent weeks at the dump searching in vain for the missing body. None of the men wanted to be here, but duty was duty. Nelson didn't know how much longer he could stand it.

Nelson and Simpson joined the lines of cops separating trash from hospital waste, tin cans from dirty diapers, and then casting it all aside. He stood in the city's solid waste cesspool, doggedly searching for the body of a person he had never seen before.

Nelson dragged the rake across the surface of the dump, thinking of nothing in particular except getting through another shift in Hell.

All of the cops expected the worst if they were to find Lori. It had been thirty days now, and surely the summer heat had taken its toll on the the tissue and bone that had made up a human body. Would they find only skeletal remains? Would the body be mostly liquid? The dump was a place where things decomposed rapidly by design. Would there be anything left? How long would they search before they gave up?

Early fall in Utah is magnificent. The mountains turn bright orange, and the first snows reach the higher elevations, closing roads until spring. Yet in the Salt Lake Valley, there are still vestiges of summer as the bright western sun beats down on a land in confusion, not really desert, but not an Alpine valley either. The air is thin at a mile high, and the light is relentless.

The rake, its spokes turned at a 90-degree angle from the handle, caught something. Nelson looked down to see what he had snagged.

It looked like another bag from a barbershop. The men had become accustomed to seeing the sacks filled with blond, gray, brown, black, dry, greasy, and dishwater-colored hair. Salt Lake City was filled with barber and beauty salons. In fact, Utah is a good market for beauty products, and hairdressers can make a good living from the vanity of young Mormon girls determined to catch a returning missionary.

Nelson pulled the rake across the plastic bag to expose more of the hair, picking its loose fold and opening it upon the ground. The hair looked familiar, like some he had seen recently, perhaps in a photograph. The connection came instantly thunderous in its meaning.

He briefly stood there wearing a mask over his nose to help stifle the odor that never seemed to go completely away. Nelson wore a ball cap to shield his face from the sun, and sunglasses to protect his eyes. On his hands he had gloves to protect him from a snag that might bring infection. Rubber boots with two-inch-thick soles protecting his feet; and, across his chest and back, he wore an orange smock with a yellow stripe running up and down to distinguish him and his fellow searchers from others in the landfill.

They could just as easily have been a chain gang on work detail. They were cops, and J. R. Nelson was the cop of the moment. As he pulled the fold back, uncertain of what he would find, he saw tissue, then bone in the hair, recognition becoming more certain by the nanosecond. Then he saw Lori Hacking's jawbone and teeth.

"I've found her!" he shouted to Detective Jim Prior, standing thirty yards from him.

The investigator walled casually over to Nelson. He expected another false alarm.

It was 8:30 a.m.

A crowd of officers quickly gathered. The team soon came to the conclusion that what they were looking at was what was left of a beautiful girl named Lori Hacking.

It had taken Nelson and the other cops more than thirty days on and off since July 30 to sift through 4,600 tons of garbage to find the 35 pounds of human remains.

In life, Lori had weighed 113 pounds.

Radio waves crackled as cops on the dump detail notified their supervisors and Chief Rick Dinse at headquarters that the team had uncovered the body. The search could well be over. In Bob Stott's office there was cause for encouragement. While he and Athay had reached unspoken agreement that there wouldn't be a trial, at least now there might be a corpus delicti.

Making a positive identification was now a priority as the body was transported down California Street and into Salt Lake City proper to the office of the medical examiner, where Lori's dental records were waiting.

Within hours, there was a match. The team who had spent over thirty days digging in the city dump had found the body of Lori Hacking. She would not suffer the indignity of a final resting place where tin cans were her tombstone and plastic bags were the flowers.

Lori was going home to Orem.

Bob Stott was among the first to hear of the result of the "autopsy." The remains were indeed his murder victim, but they provided scant information. The medical examiner hadn't even been able to determine cause of death. Had Mark Hacking not confessed, the case would have been thin indeed, Stott acknowledged. He wondered if his team could have even secured a conviction as he recalled that until Mark had told his brothers that he'd shot his wife, the police and prosecutors believed that he had strangled her.

The autopsy would have left them to continue operating from that theory—there was no evidence of a gunshot wound to the head, because there was virtually no head left, only bone fragments. The garbage compactor had been efficient in crushing the contents of the Dumpster where Mark had deposited his wife.

In the prosecutor's mind, only two things clearly linked Mark Hacking to the murder of his wife: his confession, and the receipt that he had clumsily left in his car.

Had he kept his mouth shut to his brothers, Mark Hacking might very easily have gotten away with murder.

Eraldo Soares, eloquent, emotional, needed something more. He needed closure with the dump. He asked to be taken to the exact site where Nelson had found what was left of his daughter's body.

It was a usual gorgeous fall day in Zion as Eraldo emerged from the car, his feet tentatively stepping on the filthy surface, frightened that he might be stepping on other remains of his daughter that had not been found by the police.

Eraldo Soares hated being in the dump, yet he had to be there. He looked at the spot where Nelson had caught the bag with hair inside.

He came because he believed he owed the trip to Lori. He looked at the spot, deposited a flower, and prayed.

Eraldo Soares had fulfilled his obligation.

There was plenty of talk behind the scenes, speculation running rampant that Mark Hacking would be on his way to the prison at Point of the Mountain around Christmas, the plea bargain a present to his parents.

But what bargain? What cards did Athay have to play in his client's behalf?

None.

The idea of prosecuting Hacking under the fetal homicide law had vanished with the decomposition of Lori's remains.

Talk of a deal was among courthouse outsiders, not the insiders near Hacking's lawyer and Bob Stott. Some who were close to the case were distressed at how it was being treated by the prosecution.

Lori's family in particular was uneasy about the way the district attorney's office was handling the case.

"I didn't think he [Stott] really cared much about this case. I was never really impressed with the DA's office and their handling of the case or how they dealt with us," Paul Soares later recalled.

The mainstream press did little more than watch for filings at the courthouse, and the irreverent *City Weekly* was uncharacteristically quiet throughout the search for Lori Hacking and the confession of her husband. Finally, the paper's editors could contain themselves no longer when it came time to publish the annual "Best Of " issue, giving the case a tout in its awards section as the "Best News Story Ad Nauseum."

Now that Lizzy Smart is safe, sound and surprising those who pictured her as a mere child plucking away at a giant harp, local media outlets grabbed on the next, best tragedy: Lori Hacking. Once the search for a missing pregnant woman turned into a search for her remains, constant case follow-ups grew tiring. Yes, it was all very sordid and shocking—Mark Hacking lied about his education, allegedly shot his wife when she found out, wrapped her in a mattress and dropped it in a dumpster. He then sent volunteers off to search in all directions, all hoping to find Lori alive. But once the truth came out, did we really need daily updates from the county landfill? Cadaver dog reports? National talk-show appearances? Enough!

The town's plucky youth-oriented alternative paper echoed the grown-up daily *Salt Lake Tribune* in its desire for the case, and the national media attention it generated, to go away once and for all. Deep down, even Zion's most liberal news outlet preferred that the city's tarnished underbelly be seen only as far as State Street, and not very much at that.

The Scott M. Matheson Courthouse sits comfortably across State Street from Salt Lake's ornate Victorian City and County Building. Seated there are five judges of the Supreme Court (in Utah, the title for those holding jobs on appellate benches is judge, not justice), seven appellate court judges, five juvenile judges, and twenty-two judges functioning at the trial court level. The judges do their work in thirty-seven modern but ornate courtrooms trimmed in cherry wood.

The building is imposing, containing 420,000 feet of workspace, including the courtrooms. It is 120 feet from the top of the rotunda to the floor.

The building is named for former Utah Governor Scott Matheson, who claimed that the reason he ran for the state's highest office was to stack the courts, saying: "I was always very interested in judges. The chance to make an impact on the judicial bench . . . was one of the main reasons for me to run for governor."

The building is filled with art with a distinctly Utah flavor, purchased by funds made up of one percent of the building's construction cost. The powerful Utah Arts Council, one of the most progressive in the nation, pushed the provision through the state legislature.

By modern courthouse standards, the Matheson building is stunning. The fund has produced colored stenciling in the rotunda, the paintings in its main gallery, the windows and painting in the Supreme Court, sculptured lamps on State Street and even the name on the front of the building. Private funding added further fine touches such as additional stenciling and beautiful but practical stone flooring. The total cost of the courthouse was $79 million, and it took almost three years to build.

Mark Hacking's case was destined for the Third District, trial courts serving Salt Lake, Tooele, and Summit Counties.

By the luck of the draw, his fate was assigned to no-nonsense Judge Denise Lindberg. She and her family had come to the United States after fleeing Fidel Castro's oppressive regime.

Utah Governor Mike Leavitt had appointed the Cuban American jurist to the bench. Courthouse gossips say that the appointment was a letdown to her. Socially prominent and brilliant—with a résumé and Rolodex to match any lawyer in Utah—Lindberg had expected an appellate bench, maybe even a seat on the state's highest court. It wasn't meant to be, at least not for a while.

Lindberg got her degrees from the University of Utah and graduated magna cum laude from Brigham Young University where she served on the *Law Review* as articles editor.

From law school, the attractive lawyer clerked for Monroe McKay on the U.S. Court of Appeals for the 10th District, then worked for Justice Sandra Day O'Connor at the U.S. Supreme Court.

After rubbing shoulders with "The Supremes," Lindberg practiced appellate and healthcare law in the nation's capital. She returned to Utah in 1994 to serve as in-house counsel for a healthcare company.

Lindberg, a Republican, centered her practice on advising health plans and managed care companies on regulatory matters that affect their bottom line. She has served as the state bar's co-chair of its healthcare committee.

She is married to another lawyer.

Lindberg is a Master of the Bench with the American Inns of Court, an organization of judges, lawyers, and law professors loosely based on the British legal apprenticeship program.

But despite her considerable accomplishments, Lindberg has been a disappointment on the bench according to some courthouse sources who have watched her during her seven years as a judge.

Mark Hacking's only solace was that Lindberg was a practicing Mormon. The judge's religious faith could be either good news or bad news for him.

One task of defense attorneys is the ultimate confrontation with a client in which the lawyer must tell the pure unvarnished truth. He must bring a semblance of reality to an otherwise unreal situation.

The client sits in the sterile confines of jail, institutionalized maybe for the first time in his life. In some cases, the client, unschooled in the law, has deluded himself that his lawyer is a magic man who holds the keys to the jail. In some communities, money-hungry lawyers bent upon a volume practice, have erected billboards along busy expressways advertising those keys, perpetuating the myth that a lawyer can free the guilty, no matter how heinous the crime.

The O.J. Simpson case helped perpetuate that hope. The late Johnnie Cochran, the able California criminal defense attorney, was aided by a blue-ribbon team of lawyers who pecked the seed of doubt into the bark of certainty that the famed NFL running back was guilty. Cochran did not hesitate to play the race card. Despite a persuasive case by the prosecution, the defense prevailed, allowing Simpson to spend a wasted life on his NFL pension going from golf course to golf course surrounded by hangers on.

O.J. Simpson is every guilty defendant's hero, and Cochran the magic man who saved him.

The achievement of the Simpson team in springing O.J. is a rare example of magic in the pit—brilliant lawyering swaying a jury in favor of a seemingly guilty defendant.

Despite his considerable skills and decades in the courtroom, Gilbert Athay didn't have a prayer of obtaining freedom for Mark Hacking.

The killing was bad enough, but Athay knew that under the right circumstances, even that could be surmounted. Even a confession, as in Texas's Durst case, could possibly be overcome. But surface appearances, though substantively superficial, can count for a lot in court proceedings. The lies that Mark had told Lori were utterly despicable. That, combined with the defendant's imposing physical presence, made a Hacking defense difficult, at best, and likely impossible.

The time had come for Athay to cement the groundwork he had begun laying months before. Early on, he'd cautioned Mark not to get his hopes up. Now, he needed to prepare his client for the inevitable—the fact that both he and Stott had known from the beginning: There would be no trial for Mark Hacking. He would go to prison, potentially for the rest of his life.

As Mark Hacking sat in the Salt Lake County Jail adjusting to life behind bars, the case faded from the nation's headlines. Quickly he learned that he had to find something to do to pass the time. He decided to write a book about what really happened.

The task was therapy, nothing more—and Mark had almost certainly seen the benefits of therapeutic writing in his work at the university psychiatric hospital.

It is a way of purging the conscience, often used by 12-steppers confronting their demons head-on by putting down on paper every sin they had ever committed against other people.

Whether Hacking came up with the project on his

own, or was doing it on the suggestion of Athay or a family member, the writing almost certainly would help settle the guilt a normal person would feel in his situation. Whether Mark Hacking was normal was a matter for debate.

Mark Hacking is a dreamer, and it is entirely possible that he so deluded himself that he believed his work would be a best seller. The likelihood of anything being published authored by the country's most infamous liar was remote because of Utah's Son of Sam law.

The Orem City cemetery sits at the base of a grassy slope that runs gently up Mount Timpanogos, site of one of the nation's most breathtaking hiking trails. For those hardy enough to trudge along the path, spectacular beauty awaits. Nearby, Provo Canyon bisects the Wasatch Range as it climbs ever higher and higher into the mountains. The fashionable make a short drive, turning off I-15, and into the canyon to play at Sundance, the ski-resort home of actor Robert Redford. When they do, they pass within a mile of the final resting place of a young mother-to-be named Lori Hacking.

The cemetery is small, with a circular drive around its perimeter, bisected by another drive to accommodate funerals and pallbearers who would otherwise have to carry a heavy, body-laden casket a considerable distance. At its rear, a memorial to war dead lends a mantle of valor to the place.

On Saturday, October 9, 2004, those chosen to carry Lori Hacking's thirty-five pounds of remains and her silver-gray casket would not have far to trudge across the closely cropped cemetery grass. Her gravesite was dug on a sun-drenched spot near the road. The press held at bay for the moment, all Utah watched and cared as the much-traveled bones of Lori Hacking were laid to rest in a ceremony lasting less than an hour.

Lori's brother, Paul, held his arm around their mother, Thelma, who sat next to her former husband, Eraldo, in the front row under a blue funeral canopy. A uniformed cop stood near the end of the casket.

As the casket sat above the open grave catching the last reflections of sun to ever hit its polished surface, a spray of red roses lay on its lid, softening the horror of what was inside.

J. R. Nelson was there. The veteran cop was taking it all very hard.

Paul Soares was the first to speak, heaping praise on the cops.

"You dedicated and brave officers who performed your terrible task without ever giving up, day after day—how can we possibly thank you for giving us this sacred gift?"

Thelma and Eraldo, and Janet and Doug Hacking had remained close throughout the ordeal of the search and its conclusion. The Soareses had made it clear that they didn't blame the family of their daughter's husband for what he had done.

Eraldo Soares told the crowd of his gratitude in having Lori with him and the family for twenty-seven years. Yet bitterness was impossible to conceal for him as he dedicated the grave of his daughter. He refused to use the name *Hacking*, instead referring to her as Lori Soares.

The family then unfurled a banner saying, "Lori is home, Your prayers are answered THANK YOU The Soares Family."

At the end, each mourner filed past the silver casket and placed long-stemmed roses on the lid.

Janet Hacking, Mark's mother, embraced Thelma Soares, wiping away a tear from the woman's cheek.

A poem summed up the short life of Lori Hacking. It described an all-American girl grown to womanhood. A copy was presented to the cops who'd searched for her. Many of them—tough, hardened, world-weary, cynical, and even callous—cried.

Lori

You are a small town girl with big city sophistication
You are California cool and Las Vegas excitement
But also, Washington, D.C. intellect and New York chic

You are summer flip flops, bright, vibrant colors and
   basking in the sun
You are spring with great ideas constantly blooming in
   your head
You are gorgeous smile radiating warmth on a cold winter's day
You are autumn, never afraid to change or to try something new

You are birthday celebrations at The Old Spaghetti Factory in Trolley Square

You are KBER 101 music and a concert in Park City

You are Diet Cokes at Will's Pit Stop, extra large of course

You are cruising around town in your blue bug sporting "Daddy bought it but I got it"

You are rollerblading trips up the canyon

You are long conversations on the phone and weekend sleepovers

You are Training Table cheese fries, Wendy's Frostys, and Stan's shakes

You are V-neck T-shirts and reverse fit jeans

You are shopping sprees at Lerners always sporting the latest fashions

You are hoop earrings and silver necklaces of every sort

You are hair straightening for hours at a time

You are a larger-than-life personality bounding from a petite frame

You are the host and the life of the party always good for a laugh

You are teenage girl fights . . . not always sure of the reason

You are a roll of the eyes . . . which tells so much

You are a balanced checkbook and a carefully organized closet

You are goals to be set . . . then achieved

You are beautiful in every way

You are excellence and perfection, outspoken and determined, feisty and fun

You are a friend to all

You are unconditional love . . . a best friend who is always
   there
We will always love you, Lori. We are blessed and grateful to be your friends,
Forever

Chapter Fifteen

Within days, a marker denoted the place where a once-vibrant girl who had been the toast of Orem lay. The grave could not be distinguished from the street, for the tombstone sat low and flush with the ground. Its gray granite face scored with her name, Lori Kay Hacking, as well as her birth and death dates, and in italics, "Our Angel Baby." To the right of the inscription lay a rose carved in stone, its petals touching a heart enclosing the words, "We love you."

An oval color photograph of the dead woman was embedded into the granite. Lori's trademark long brown hair, which had identified the remains for Officer Nelson, hung in luxuriant tresses from her head.

Eraldo couldn't stomach the name *Hacking* appearing on his daughter's tombstone for time and all eternity. Within weeks, it would be changed to Lori Kay Soares, and under the name, Eraldo's pet nickname for her, "Filhinha" was now etched into the gray stone. The translation, "little daughter."

From the moment of her burial, a steady stream of the curious came to Lori's grave. In death, she was the public figure she had never been in life—and never wanted to be. Lori now belonged to the world, a tragic figure—a memory that would eventually fade until hers was just another grave in the small cemetery abutting the Wasatch Mountains, and the visitors no longer came.

There was a change in the appearance of Mark Hacking that went far beyond the shaved head, mustache and goatee. Gone was the open-faced red-headed kid with brushed-back hair and an ever-present smile on his face.

Mark Hacking was now a con, a prisoner, a jailbird. His face was hard, and even world-weary. Where once his eyebrows had been spread and wide-set over his nose, the red hair almost indistinguishable from his fair complexion, they had now narrowed.

Mark's hair color had changed as well. His mustache and beard, as well as the eyebrows, were now dark, almost the color of Lori's. The dark eyebrows knitted together in a frown that said everything there was to say regarding his prospects for the future.

With inevitable certainty, Mark Hacking followed the case of Scott Peterson, accused in California of killing his pregnant wife. With his conviction in December, and his ultimate death sentence under the Golden State's fetal homicide law, Hacking began to bask in the limelight bouncing off Peterson's case into Utah.

In a letter obtained by *The National Enquirer*, Hacking wrote a friend shortly after Peterson's trial that "Apparently Scott Peterson had an affair and this played a big part in his trial. Many people like to compare his case and mine."

Hacking smugly believed that after his admission of guilt in court, "The Peterson case will not affect what will happen with me—at least not in the courtroom. I am sure it has and will affect public sentiment."

Jail can be a terribly lonely place to spend any length of time at all, particularly for a young man shielded from the hardscrabble world of the common criminal because of a privileged upbringing. Naturally outgoing, Mark Hacking made friends even in the close quarters of the Salt Lake County lockup.

Of all the acquaintances he made in jail, the most strange was the man who called himself Emmanuel, the street preacher and prophet Brian David Mitchell, who spent his days in confinement in a cell along the same section as Mark Hacking.

Both now infamous, the two struck up a relationship through music. Mitchell, the alleged kidnapper and rapist of Elizabeth Smart, would sing hymns to drown out the noise made by raucous street gangs engaged in verbal battles among themselves.

By March, Hacking summoned the courage to challenge Mitchell to a singing competition, and the alleged rapist accepted.

Hacking bragged in a letter sent out of the jail that because he was kept so close to the Manson lookalike in his 10×12 foot cell, he might be summoned to testify in upcoming hearings to determine if the former Smart family employee was fit to stand trial.

The admitted murderer did not reveal in his letters who won the competition, Mitchell singing his hymns, or Mark Hacking's rendition of songs he learned as a child such as "Row, Row, Row Your Boat."

There is a fair degree of certainty that both contestants annoyed the street gangs.

Mark Hacking was making other friends in jail, friendships and familial relationships that he could carry to prison with him. In the lock-up, he met a third-rate robber who he befriended by making a phone call to the man's aunt. Word got back to the man's family, two more members of whom were charged in the same robbery as the accused felon Hacking had befriended. One got off, counting his blessings that he had hired Ron Yengich. Another brother didn't fare so well, drawing a public defender for his case. He was to be sentenced to 5 years to life in prison the same afternoon Mark was to face Lindburg his final time.

His crime?

The man would go to jail for a substantial portion of his life for stealing a VCR from a Salt Lake City retailer. Zero tolerance was working in Utah.

But among prisoners, little kindnesses count. Mark Hacking was already racking up points among his fellow inmates. He might have a friend to go through prison orientation with.

The politics of Utah, often rambunctious, did not abate as Hark Hacking sat amusing himself in the Salt Lake County Jail.

Mayor Nancy Workman had been acquitted in a bruising skirmish with DA David Yocom. It had taken its toll on the lawyer. He told Stott and his associates he wanted to retire to southern Utah. The bruises were deep.

For his part, Stott expressed no desire to run for the soon-to-be-vacant office. He was happy to finish his career as a prosecutor, working in the pit of a courtroom. Administrative work held no sweetness for him.

Salt Lake City's irrepressible Mayor Rocky Anderson delighted in tweaking the noses of the city's establishment, much of it sitting in offices near Temple Square. Loved by the press and much of the public, the mayor consistently made appointments that were controversial in the eyes of almost half of the population of the city he led. Anderson's political picks were chosen not for their faith (somewhat unusual in Zion), or their heterosexual orientation, age, gender, or economic condition, but by how they best could fit into the job which they were appointed to do. A full third of his staff and appointments are minorities.

The long months of incarceration were taking a terrible toll on the family members on both sides. In particular, Paul, Lori's affable brother, felt the tug of Mark Hacking, sometimes saying that he felt like a marionette, and his sister's killer was pulling the strings. He was familiar with law enforcement work. For six years, he had served as a police dispatcher in Utah County before returning to California. His knowledge of how things are done had helped him interpret what was going on behind closed doors to the family. Yet the knowledge hadn't made things any easier for him.

Paul, now a compliance officer with a mutual fund company, and his family made the twelve-hour trip across the desert from their California home to attend important events related to the case. At other times, he responded to calls from reporters asking for comment, and appeared on early morning television programs without complaining. His cell phone only stopped ringing when he shut the thing off.

The big man, now studying to become a paralegal, was white hot at his former brother-in-law. The anger was compounded by having to live through the events that were inevitably an outgrowth of the murder, such as the trips he was forced to make to attend hearings. At those appearances, Mark never faced the audience, never looked Paul in the eye. Paul felt it was his obligation to Lori to be there on her behalf.

Lori Soares Hacking was born on New Year's Eve. On the one hand, the entire world celebrates your birthday if you come into the world on that particular date. On the other, you are technically almost a year older than people who happenstance and biology caused them to be born a day later.

For Mark Hacking, the date brought with it a sadness he had never felt before for what he had done. He confided to a friend that her birthday was "one of the toughest times."

In another passage from a series of letters to a pen pal in the outside world published by *The National Enquirer*, Hacking wrote, "Every day the realization of what I have done and the people I have hurt haunts me with more and more guilt and grief than I knew was humanly possible." He continued saying that at times he was "overwhelmed with grief and wanted to cry."

Mark knew that he was likely to spend much of the

rest of his life in prison. He also knew that he must again hone his skills at deception, because in prison, being good at it could mean survival. He passed the time thinking about his prospects, writing his book on the murder, and reading.

He checked books out from the prison library. His reading habits proved to be eclectic: *Anna Karenina, Beloved, The Color Purple, Animal Farm, Around the World in Eighty Days, 1984, Gone With the Wind,* and *Lolita.*

Hacking also had plenty of time to feel sorry for himself, yet he put an optimistic, if unoriginal, slant on his situation in a letter to a friend: "When life gives you lemons, make lemonade!"

Hacking was not without admirers in the free world. "I still get crazy mail from crazy people," he wrote. "This adds a little comic relief to the situation."

On April 6, 2005, Mark Hacking was driven from the jail through bright spring sunlight into a dark garage in the basement of the Scott M. Matheson Courthouse. He was then taken to a holding cell to wait for Judge Denise Lindberg to convene court.

Athay had long ago told his client of the options facing him. None were good. He could face the judge alone and take his chances on mercy. He could stand before a jury and listen as Stott described how Mark had put a gun to the head of his sleeping wife and pulled the trigger. He could cop a plea, take the mandatory 5-years–to–life sentence and take his chances that the parole board would smile upon him as a first offender and let him out of prison ahead of schedule.

Early on, both men knew the option Mark Hacking would choose.

The tiny courtroom sits near the end of a wide hallway with tan and cream marble tiles on its floor. At either end, huge windows stare out at snow-capped mountains. To the east, the hulk of the gothic City and County Building dominates the street.

The hallway is lined with benches, hard benches without a single cushion.

In high-profile cases, courtrooms across the nation fill with the curious, members of the public addicted to the pull and tug of watching lawyers at trial. Yet for Mark's penultimate hearing, only his family, a handful of Lori's co-workers, members of law enforcement, and the press were on hand to jam the tiny courtroom. On one of the benches, a handicapped man sat waiting to be admitted to the room to watch the proceedings. Bailiffs declined him entry due to lack of space.

Lindberg's courtroom is tiny. Bailiffs sternly turn away those without court-issued credentials. Even three friends of Lori Hacking from Wells Fargo, among the last people to see her alive, were refused admission at first. Finally, they were admitted to take the last three remaining seats in the room.

The judge's bench sits in a corner of the room. Behind the jury box, travel posters hang, picturing the scenic beauty of Mount Timpanogos, Canyonlands National Park, and Zion National Park.

At 1:40 p.m., nine members of Mark Hacking's family were led into the courtroom and instructed to sit on the second and third rows to the left of the aisle. The contingent, led by Dr. Douglas Hacking, sat down quietly. Pretty Janet Hacking, Mark's mother, sat next to her husband. The family, well-washed, attractive and proper, looked for the entire world like they should appear on an LDS recruiting poster. One of the young men wore sandals, unaware of proper dress for a visit to a courtroom.

After they were seated, Gilbert Athay walked into the room exuding the confidence of the top lawyer that he is.

Five minutes later, Eraldo and his new family were brought in, followed by his son, Paul. Thelma Soares, wearing khaki pants, a white shirt, and light blue sweater, then entered, accompanied by members of her church. Lori's parents were seated on benches across the aisle from the Hackings.

The formality of the setting evoked earlier happier times for the parents, a time in a large white building in Bountiful where their children were joined for time and all eternity in marriage. The couples continued to feel warmth for each other. Doug and Janet Hacking embraced Lori's father and mother, crying.

As members of the press began to fill the room, six burly Salt Lake County deputies stood idly inside the bar, the rail that separates the public area from the business end of a courtroom, as they awaited the proceedings. At 1:48 p.m., one of them strode to the back of the courtroom and in a highly unusual procedure, locked the doors, just as Lori's three co-workers squeezed into the last three seats on the back bench.

Dr. Douglas Hacking nervously fumbled with his seating credentials as he held the hand of his wife. On the front row, Eraldo Soares stared ahead, while his former wife sat directly behind him.

Savvy reporters quickly guessed that they were about to witness a guilty plea on the part of Mark Hacking, because there were no documents lying on either counsel table—yet none could report it because the doors were now locked.

Bob Stott entered holding a coffee cup, and exchanged pleasantries with his adversary, Gil Athay. For both men, it was a situation they'd been in countless times in countless courtrooms during their decades before the bench. At 1:57 p.m., deputies called Athay to a side door opposite the jury box. Mark Hacking had arrived to cop his plea.

The 29-year-old inmate was escorted into the room wearing a beige jumpsuit emblazoned with the words SALT LAKE COUNTY JAIL.

Athay hadn't tried to clean him up, to make him more presentable to the judge or any potential jury that might be required by the proceedings. Mark Hacking had lost weight, and his complexion had taken on the pallor of one who seldom sees the sun. He still sported a shaved head, and had now shaved his goatee and mustache.

The judge took her place on the bench and brought the proceeding to order.

"We have reached a resolution on this matter," Stott announced to the court.

Mark stood looking at the judge, his hands still cuffed behind his back, as she explained that a guilty plea in the case would automatically necessitate his giving up any right to appeal. She told him that he would face 5 years to life in prison, with an additional year tacked on because he had committed his crime with a gun. She then asked him to tell the court exactly what he'd done when he'd committed the crime that would send him to prison.

"I intentionally shot Lori Hacking in the head with a .22 rifle on July nineteenth," he said as he stared straight ahead.

Now looking at the back of the man who had killed her daughter and unborn grandchild, Thelma Soares could no longer contain the grief. She sobbed. Across the aisle, Janet Hacking involuntarily leaned against her husband as she heard her son confess that he was a murderer.

There was now no mystery as to the fate of Mark Hacking. He was destined for a life behind bars at the prison at Point of the Mountain near Draper.

The moment Mark Hacking was escorted from the courtroom, the press bolted from the jury box where the bailiff had seated them, eager to call their editors with the news that Utah's most famous criminal had pled guilty. At the end of the long hallway, an area had been set up to hold a news conference.

Lori's mother, father, and brother now came before the familiar microphones to speak.

Eraldo, increasingly respected by the police and press for his eloquence and passion, summed up the feeling of the family.

"When he said that, it was like a knife going through my heart."

Behind him, the Hacking family left the courtroom quietly.

Meanwhile, television crews were already setting up in the office of Gilbert Athay across the street from the courthouse.

Bob Stott sat in his office fielding calls from the media. The senior prosecutor has a corner of the Broadway building, befitting his status as the Salt Lake lawyer in charge of sending murderers away to prison. His walls are covered with art: a courtroom artist's rendering of Stott standing at a lectern; a photo of his large family; a pillow with the quote, " 'I cannot live without books' —Thomas Jefferson to John Adams, 1815." And rows of books line the top and bottom shelves of a bookcase filled with mementos including a tennis trophy.

On his desk, Stott keeps a bamboo back scratcher, which he claims is used by his guests more often than himself.

He looked down at State Street, recalling the meeting with Athay there months before.

"I knew there would be a plea," he said as the phone rang. He closed his eyes when speaking with journalists about a case, lost in complete concentration, lest he say the wrong thing. On first meeting, he rarely looked at a reporter directly. Eye contact comes as journalists earn the veteran prosecutor's trust.

Stott picked up the phone. It was a booker from a network morning show asking that he appear as a guest the following day. He told them to be at his home in Bountiful the following morning before daybreak.

The next day, two young women drove up to the cemetery at the base of the mountain in Orem. They exited their car and began looking for the grave of the pregnant woman who had been featured so prominently in the news the day before. The two searched the small area where the meager remains of Lori Hacking lay buried, finally finding the grave. They looked down reverently, lost in thoughts of the woman whose bones had been found in the city dump after being tossed away like garbage.

Toward noon, a large man got out of a car, walked to the grave, knelt, and prayed. A news photographer stood by to record the scene. Paul had come to Orem to be with his sister.

The Bountiful Temple gleamed as white as Wasatch peaks in winter the day after Mark Hacking told the world that he had shot his wife in the head as she slept. Couples and their families, dressed for a wedding, left their cars in the large landscaped parking lot on the north side of the building and approached the elegant entrance as Mark and Lori must have done not many years before.

Others parked their cars as well, coming to perform their Temple ordinances, the ritual devout Mormons enact to stay in the good graces of their Church.

Inside of the great white building high above America's Salt Lake, they would perform the secret ceremony sealing them for time and all eternity as Joseph Smith had designed it a century and a half before.

Far below, the once-shimmering lake looked more like an ugly coastal salt marsh. America's great inland salt sea, all 1,700 square miles of it, had dropped almost six feet, leaving it little more than half its normal size. A six-year drought had left the Salt Lake Valley bone dry, devoid of life, as far as the eye could see. Inside the Salt Lake County Jail there was plenty of water to be had for Mark Hacking and his fellow inmates. It was the food he complained about, writing to his jailhouse pen pal of nine months, quipping, "I learned that I have lost 13 pounds since I arrived in jail. Perhaps I could start a new fad called the jailhouse diet. It would mostly consist of eating bologna and pacing in small circles."

Eraldo Soares was troubled by the way a sentence for murder was administered in Utah. The California man didn't like the fact that when Mark Hacking received his punishment from Judge Lindberg on June 6, he would likely be told that he would spend 6 years to life in the state prison.

Six years?

The thought of it was appalling, despite the fact that chances of such a brief stay at Point of the Mountain were remote. Lori's father began to think, to contemplate what it would take to change the law on behalf of his and other families who had lost loved ones.

Eraldo wanted a mandatory and lengthy sentence for future Mark Hackings who were found guilty of killing their partners.

Soares was on firm ground in proposing such a law in Utah. Utah's murder rate for domestic partners was 23 percent higher than the national average.

If it were to catch on, such new legislation could be called Lori's Law.

◆ ◆ ◆

Mark Hacking sat in a jail cell with little more to do than write pages of a book that would likely never be published, sing songs with the alleged kidnapper of Elizabeth Smart, and complain about the food. He had now pleaded guilty and he knew that he was likely to spend a substantial portion of his future behind bars.

In reality, unless something radical were to change Utah politics, the lock-up would likely be torn down because the land at the end of Point of the Mountain was becoming far too valuable to house the likes of Mark Hacking. The Wasatch Front was growing rapidly and the municipal planning principle of "highest and best use" for the property would almost certainly be a focus soon. As one of the most desirable places to live in the country, the land occupied by the prison bordering I-15 and its quick access to the commercial center of Salt Lake City was ripe for development.

Just up the highway to the north, developers had built a huge number of tract houses on the side of a mountain.

No, while Mark was undoubtedly going to the state prison in Draper, it was a safe bet that he would eventually be transferred to a newer, more modern prison yet to be built.

Time weighed heavily on his hands as the now-confessed killer awaited his sentencing on June 6, 2005.

Just before the date arrived, Hacking wrote the Soares family admitting that he had known Lori was pregnant. He had kept the fact that he was aware of her condition secret until after his guilty plea in order to escape Utah's fetal homicide law.

Lori's brother, Paul, told *The National Enquirer*, with whom he was in frequent contact throughout the case, that he hoped his brother-in-law would "rot in hell for killing my sister and her unborn child."

Eraldo Soares did more than hope. He sent Mark's letter to the Salt Lake County District Attorney's Office. Stott and his team reviewed it and concluded that it was not sufficient to bring additional charges against Mark.

"From a legal standpoint it adds nothing to the charges," Stott said. "Not only was it produced after the guilty plea, but it would not be sufficient evidence to base another murder charge or a capital [murder] charge.

"The burden is on the state to prove beyond a reasonable doubt that a second person was killed. We would base such charges only upon medical evidence, either before she was murdered, or evidence from the autopsy. Neither existed.

"Evidence of Mark's belief that he killed his unborn child is not sufficient evidence that he actually had an unborn child that was killed," Stott continued.

June 6 came as kids across Utah enjoyed their first day of summer vacation. But they wouldn't be heading to the pool. Spring had finally brought rain to Utah, breaking the drought that had devastated the state since 1999.

The morning broke, gray, colorless, wet, and unseasonably cold. In fact, Salt Lake City was enduring a deluge of biblical proportions as workers clogged the freeways and byways trying to get to the office. Two hours before Mark Hacking's sentencing hearing was scheduled to begin, the temperature still hovered at 44 degrees, and forecasters intimated that the thermometer wasn't likely to get past 50 for the entire day.

An observer of the case who was to attend the hearing waxed poetic, writing that "as the rain continued for hours unabated, it sometimes seemed like the heavens themselves were weeping for the angels Lori and her unborn baby."

Announcers on KSL, the news/talk AM radio giant, cautioned drivers to slow down, warning of the likelihood of hydroplaning on the streets and highways.

That morning, Broadcasting Hall of Fame air personality Doug Wright was on vacation, and subbing for him at KSL was a disc jockey who wanted to try his hand at talk radio. Mark Parsons was a twenty-five-year veteran music broadcaster. On the air, he compared his situation to a basketball player in his first NBA game being sent in to sub for Shaq.

Parsons had plenty to talk about for his first day behind the mike. KSL's Ben Winslow was stationed at the courthouse awaiting the sentencing of Mark Hacking. The local story made Parsons' job easy.

Callers overwhelmingly were disappointed that Mark Hacking was not to stand trial. They wanted him to receive the supreme penalty for killing his wife and unborn child.

One caller even suggested that Hacking's parents pay the cost of their son's incarceration. There, Parsons drew the line, confessing to his listeners that Douglas Hacking had been his pediatrician as a child, and had given him his physical exam immediately before Parsons departed on his journey as a Mormon missionary.

Yet Hacking wasn't the only topic on the town's most popular radio station. Some Utahans were more interested in talking about the morning's announcement that the U.S. Supreme Court had ruled against proponents of medical marijuana, the Tom Cruise/Katie Holmes romance and the couples' age gap, as well as the spectacle of the trial of Michael Jackson. In typical Salt Lake fashion, even on a gray, rainy, cold summer morning, the Church was ever present. The station advertised the 175th Mormon Miracle Pageant in Manti.

The lie-telling machine that was Mark Hacking now sat in a holding cell waiting what was sure to be a confrontation from Lori's family.

Mark was already depressed. He hadn't planned for his life to take this turn. If only he had never met Lori on that campout at Lake Powell. If only she hadn't charmed him, nursing the burn on his hand when he'd stupidly hurt himself fooling with the campfire . . .

State Street outside the Matheson Courthouse was filled with satellite trucks as a nation fixed its sights on Salt Lake City.

At 12:30 p.m., Mark Hacking's parents were waved past the guards on duty at the parking garage in the basement of the building, and were brought to the fourth floor. Security was tight, the tightest in anybody's memory. Never before had there been deputies stationed as far away as 200 South and Main Street, hundreds of feet behind the building and away from the entrance to the parking garage.

On the first floor, in the rotunda, seven camera stands were already set up awaiting the outcome and the inevitable news conference by the players in the case who had endured it to the end. Cable outlets across the nation waited to break into programming to carry the proceedings live.

Upstairs, Courtroom S41 was waiting. It is the first courtroom in a broad hallway belonging to the Third District's courts. Normally, Judge Sheila McCleve presided there, but she had given up the space briefly to Lindberg because of the room's larger seating area and overflow rooms for media to watch the proceedings on closed-circuit television.

At 1:08 p.m., Thelma Soares arrived on the floor wearing a light beige jacket/skirt suit with matching shoes and a teal-colored blouse. The mother of Lori Hacking wore small silver earrings. The ravenous television media immediately surrounded her. Even a snatch of something different from a story that had run just an hour ago was welcome, a tiny morsel to feed the television news appetite.

There was nothing anyone could do to stop the intrusion of the cameras into their lives. They could only escape when the doors of the courtroom closed behind them. Mark Hacking had forever changed both sets of parents' lives. Besides taking Lori from them, he had also destroyed their privacy.

As 2 p.m. approached, six burly deputies from the Salt Lake County Sheriff's Department took their places. Utah courts had long ago recognized that sending a man to prison did not always go smoothly or peacefully. They were ready for anything.

In the first row, directly behind the prosecution

table, the Soares family took their places as Thelma looked around the courtroom making a mental note of people she knew.

Prosecutor Bob Stott stepped from behind the bar to greet her warmly.

He then returned to the trial area, joined his "second chair," Angela Micklos and defense attorney Gil Athay and the three lawyers left the room.

Moments later, they returned, followed by the judge. When everybody had taken their seats and the room had become silent, Mark Hacking was ready to face the court for his sentence.

He no longer resembled the joking and klutzy dreamer as he was brought into the courtroom wearing a bulletproof vest and shackles.

Mark Hacking's entire family was still in a daze, disbelief on their faces that this son of privilege was soon to be told that he would immediately be sent to prison, perhaps for the rest of his life.

Lori was gone, the permanence of her plight etched on a gray tombstone in Orem. Final. Over.

They rose one at a time to speak to the judge, who now must pronounce sentence on their son and brother. The sentence would be mandatory, stipulated by state law. The witness statements were simply a way in which a compassionate judge could help all sides in a case find some sort of closure.

The first speaker in the room full of people whose lives had been changed by Mark Hacking was his sister, Julie Whittaker. She had lived with her brother both before and after his Mormon mission. She told the court that despite the challenges he faced, Mark had always shown kindness and respect. Julie told the court that her brother was not a lost cause, as many in the court believed. She had loved her sister-in-law, still loved her in fact. She was certain that her brother could still do more good than damage, even if it was from behind prison walls.

Chad Hacking next described Lori with two words—"grace" and "fire"—saying that the gentle grace was in her infectious smile for him and a soft spot for those who struggled. Yet he admired her fire as well, such as her stand on issues. She would come up with sweet nicknames, and then exhibit a spitfire attitude during debate.

Chad told the court that his brother had left the family with emotional scars, saying that there was a fiery justice in his soul and then waxed biblical, comparing that justice to Hellfire, a place outside Jerusalem where humans were sacrificed to pagan gods. To many in the room, only Chad knew what he was talking about, lost in his own thoughts and theology as he addressed the court and his brother.

Chad Hacking then compared Mark's sacrifice of Lori to that mystical place, saying that he will suffer forever for what he did.

The younger brother of the murderer finished by telling the Mormon judge he now faced that after Mark had returned in disgrace from his mission to Winnipeg, he felt sorrow for the suffering he had caused the family. He'd counseled Chad on the pitfalls he had fallen into on the mission, warning his brother to avoid making the same mistakes.

Next Mark's sister Sarah faced the court, saying that she did not want to diminish the crime her brother had committed. She had been persuaded to move to the apartment complex on Lincoln Street by Mark and Lori. Uncle Mark had delighted the children by playing Nintendo with them, and Lori had been their favorite aunt.

Mark and Sarah would go on walks together, talking endlessly as they exercised. Sarah believed that her brother was under tremendous stress, using sleeping pills, and constantly exercising on a bike and running to relieve the pressure. She knew that Mark suffered from depression as well, the devastating mental condition that could devour even the most sunny personalities.

She watched Mark and Lori together and delighted in the evident love they felt for each other. That her brother could be violent toward his wife was unthinkable. In fact, despite his menacing appearance, a look that the couple found helpful in keeping tenants in line, Lori frequently described her husband as "a teddy bear."

Yet Sarah was worried, terribly worried about her brother. The week before he'd killed Lori, she and Mark had had one of their talks. In it he described for her the relief that patients of his at the hospital had when they successfully committed suicide. His depression appeared to be worsening to her.

Mark Hacking sat motionless as his siblings addressed the court, hoping against hope to lighten the load he would face in going to prison.

He didn't look at them, and instead looked downward. As speaker after speaker rose to address the judge, Mark Hacking sat mute and motionless, showing no reaction to their testimony.

Mark's sister Tiffany next spoke to the court, describing how her brother would make people laugh with his antics. Every time she saw Mark, he had a new joke at the ready. In fact, she said she had only recently seen a Halloween video in which her brother had the party in stitches.

She also described her brother as a Good Samaritan type who would do little things to help people, such as repair roofs and mow lawns if asked.

In the audience, the big brother Lori had cherished sat alone with his thoughts as the Hacking family members continued their testimony, droning on and on about what a good person Mark was.

Good Samaritan? Paul paid little attention, thinking instead of what he would say when it came time for him to give his victim's statement to the court. That would be as close as he would ever come to confronting Mark for what he had done to Lori.

Paul thought of how much his father had aged since Lori went missing and the family learned she had been murdered. Eraldo, 71, had always looked much younger than his age, working as a high school Spanish teacher until long past the normal retirement age of 65. Lori's death had taken its toll. There had been no gray in his father's hair until recently. The tragedy had aged the once-athletic educator when nothing else was able to do so.

Paul ignored Scott Hacking as he began to speak. Mark's brother told the court that the "sentencing isn't just about Lori." He continued, saying that anybody could understand feelings of hate—who wouldn't?

Mark's brother said that Mark and Lori were happy. She would sometimes go camping with her husband when that wasn't something she really wanted to do.

Scott said that Mark had lost the most. But Scott's testimony must have cut his brother deeply when he told the court that prior to Lori's murder, Mark used to play with his children. Now, after what he had done, Scott wasn't sure he would let his brother play with the kids.

Trials have a way of building to a crescendo, even when everyone knows the outcome in advance. This hearing was no different. The drama began to escalate when the first of the four parents took the stand.

Pretty Janet Hacking had looked so young from behind that some observers in the courtroom had mistakenly believed that she was another of Mark's sisters.

Nobody, with the exception of Thelma Soares, had endured more anguish than the mother of the accused. She had suffered in silence with the humiliation of having raised a son who was a coward and a murderer. Yet as she began her speech to the court, she was composed, her pain bottled up.

Janet had not been close to Thelma, although the two frequently embraced when the murder brought them together. Paul described his mother's relationship with Mark's mom as that of an acquaintance more than a friend. The two didn't even have the bond of attending the same Mormon ward, and did not live in the same stake.

Janet began to speak, talking of her sorrow and love for Lori and the family she'd left behind because of what Mark had done. Janet would have been a grandmother again, were it not for the bullet that her son had put in Lori's head. He had ended any hope of the fulfillment of the high point of Mormon culture for Lori, and by extension, Doug and Janet Hacking.

Yet a mother's love is undeniable, and Janet was no different. Her love for Mark was unconditional. She was certain he would be forgiven.

Janet deferred to "wiser hearts than mine" to administer justice and mercy.

Tears welled in the mother's eyes as she spoke. Salt Lake County deputies unsuccessfully searched the courtroom for tissues for the grieving woman, compassion overcoming their usual stony façades.

Yet Janet Hacking mounted a defense of her son, telling the court and those assembled that an accident, long alluded to by Athay, had taken a toll on her son. He had been knocked unconscious, had hurt his back, and suffered memory problems after his physical recovery.

Janet closed by telling the court that she hoped in prison her son would receive counseling, medication, and meaningful work.

While Janet Hacking pulled the heartstrings of everybody in the room, it was Douglas Hacking who revealed information that heretofore had been kept a secret by the family. Mark had tried to commit suicide by downing beer and pills the night he was found running naked in a motel parking lot, howling at the moon like a mountain wolf.

With quiet dignity, Orem's favorite pediatrician spoke to the court in quiet tones on behalf of the son who had become such a disappointment to him, saying that he still loved Mark, though hating what he'd done.

"Mark has been my son for twenty-nine years," he said. "I remember him as an infant, a toddler, doing sports, playing the violin, and overcoming challenges."

Dr. Hacking spoke of Mark's gentle side, his love of children, animals, the elderly, and the mentally ill.

His father said that Mark had always treated his parents with respect, important in any household, but a concept drilled into the soul of Mormon children.

Douglas Hacking told the court that he now better understood the concept that God loves a repentant sinner, saying that repentance had begun the night Mark tried to take his own life, leaving a note on his Palm Pilot saying, "This is justice."

The father also related how his son said that even were he to receive the death penalty, it wouldn't be enough. Moreover, Doug Hacking told the court that Mark had told family members since the previous August that his case would never be tried.

Mark had written letters to his family in which he expressed remorse at killing the "wife he loved so much."

The senior Hacking described the couple as inseparable, and always holding hands.

He then spoke of the book Mark was writing in jail. The work, continually described by the press as a "tell-all," was instead a candid autobiography for the two families so they could better understand "why this happened." Mark had no intention of publishing what he was writing, he said.

Doug Hacking said that he hoped that his son would someday be released from prison and could do more good things with his life. Yet the physician said that he was still not sure why Mark had killed the one person he loved most. Importantly, he said, Mark didn't understand either.

The physician closed asserting that it was a certainty, at least to his trained eye, that his son was suffering from psychological and mental issues as well as sleep deprivation.

Finally, Douglas Hacking told the court that his son's fate was in God's hands, and he would leave that up to the Creator.

Mark Hacking approached the podium with his lawyer on one side and a deputy on the other to prevent an unlikely escape attempt.

He wore a flack jacket, the word "PRISONER" in bold block letters on a green jail-issue bulletproof vest.

Mark spoke softly to those who had loved him most, and to some who loved him still.

Most appalling, he admitted that he had not only killed his wife, but had knowingly killed his unborn child.

Mark Hacking became more and more emotional as he stood facing the judge, saying he deserved to spend the rest of his life in prison, and that he would give a thousand lifetimes in confinement if he could change what he had done.

"She didn't do nothing but love me unconditionally, even when I didn't deserve it," he told the court, sounding curiously like a teenager.

Mark's voice soon cracked as he bowed his head and wiped tears from his eyes.

"I put them in the garbage, and they rotted out at the

landfill. I'm tormented every waking minute by what I did," he said.

Facing the judge, with his back to the audience, Mark continued, saying Lori was the greatest and that she was as beautiful inside as she was outside.

"She was the greatest thing that ever happened to me," Mark said, crying uncontrollably now.

"What would Lori want to happen now?" Mark asked. "She wouldn't care if I spent the rest of my life in prison, [but] she would care what I did with my life wherever I was. She cared about the truth. She would want me to become the man she thought I was. Lori would be concerned with her family feeling peace. If the only way for that to happen is for me to spend the rest of my life in prison, it is okay because a thousand lifetimes in prison are not enough for justice.

"Words are cheap, especially from me," Hacking continued, the words now gushing from him.

"There is no reason to believe anything I say," he continued, overcome by emotion. "From the bottom of my heart, I am so sorry for the pain I caused. I took her life, and the baby's. I put them in the garbage where they rotted at the landfill. It torments me every waking moment. I am completely okay with anything that is decided today. I probably should spend the rest of my life in prison. Thank you, Your Honor."

A skeptical audience didn't believe a word Mark Hacking said.

Gilbert Athay stood to face the court on behalf of his client. He called the case of Mark Hacking an enigma.

Athay's argument to the court was strange—a lame

attempt by a veteran lawyer to put a positive spin on what was otherwise a dreadful act.

He told the court that he had delayed the proceedings against his client's wishes.

"Mark wanted it over early," he told the court. "I believed the legal system needed more time. I accept responsibility for this decision. Thanks for listening."

Chapter Sixteen

After prosecutor Bob Stott told Judge Lindberg that the family wanted to speak, Thelma Soares walked to the podium.

When Thelma Soares stood facing the judge, her first words were powerful, telling everyone in the room that Lori Hacking had become "America's daughter." But the eloquence of her words spoke volumes. For a brief moment in a sterile courtroom in Utah, she and her former husband Eraldo had become America's parents.

Almost immediately she started crying. The moment was finally here, it had finally happened. She could now speak her mind, unleashed by the bonds of fear that she might say the wrong thing and jeopardize the state's case.

Thelma Soares could at last speak the words to Mark Hacking that she had so long wanted to say. She could speak words of comfort to his parents and siblings.

She turned to Lance and Scott Hacking, thanking them for persuading their brother to confess, and then said that Lori had loved being part of their family. Moreover, she told the Hackings that she loved them as well, saying the whole tragedy was a senseless waste of three lives.

"How can I put into words what it is like to lose my only daughter? My unborn grandchild?

"Mark made sacred covenants to love, honor, and protect them. My beloved child was torn from me by a man I entrusted her to. I have been shattered and betrayed to my very core."

Thelma's words tumbled out in a torrent of eloquence, gripping, riveting to those seated in the great room. Many looked at Mark Hacking, trying to see his reaction.

"After nearly a year, I can barely accept that he put Lori and her child into the trash," she said, anger evident in her voice.

"Only God knows the real reason why," she continued. "Mark knew that Lori would rot away, and he didn't care. He was going to commit suicide and no one would ever know where Lori was.

"Lori didn't even like to camp because she liked to be impeccably dressed, and be able to wash her hair. Now the only thing left to bury of her body was bone fragments and teeth.

"I cannot bear to see garbage trucks," she told the judge. "The sound conjures up images of her body being torn apart in the trash," she said.

"For so many years I took such good care of that body, fed and diapered it, got it immunizations, took her to the doctor, dentist, and orthodontist, clothed her, taught that body how to swim to protect it. I did things to increase her intelligence. I saw that she had worthwhile and beautiful experiences.

"Mark blew her brains to bits and threw her in the trash," Thelma Soares said, the very essence of righteous indignation.

"It shocks my senses and boggles my mind that her life was stolen by the man she loved and trusted," Thelma said. "This was not a murder committed by a street criminal or gang member.

"She loved and trusted Mark. I can only imagine Lori's disbelief and anguish when she learned their life was riddled with deception. She trusted Mark even then, not believing that Mark would blow her brains out with a gun.

"You must understand, he began to tell lies— probably as a result of a low test score or grade, but I have trouble understanding the intricate web of lies that followed."

Thelma now paid a backhanded tribute to the man who'd killed her daughter.

"He was brilliant in doing so," she said. "All of us were fooled. The morning that Mark was supposed to graduate, I heard him throwing up in the bathroom. He was so sick that I insisted on driving him to the pharmacy to pick up the prescription that his dad had called in for him.

"He still had his cap and gown the next week, and I took pictures of him in it because he missed his graduation."

Thelma now riveted the audience with her personal

experiences, relating the consummate deceptions Mark had acted out with such intricacy.

"He stored his chemistry and other books in my garage," she continued. "I helped him with his term papers. I remember him joking about how gross his gross anatomy class was. When they went back to New York for a medical school interview, he told Lori and Kathy Black about the interview. He called Lori after his interview in North Carolina and told her he was certain he would be accepted there for medical school.

"Mark told lies with such detail and expertise that I can't separate in my own life experiences anymore what was real from what wasn't. I feel like the supporting actress in a third-rate horror show. Why would killing Lori improve his lot in life? Why not kill himself?" she asked as the audience and judge listened to every painful word.

Now Thelma honed in on the upbringing of Mark Hacking.

"Mark did not have any abusive or deprived childhood, he was reared by loving and moral parents. He knew right from wrong," she asserted.

"If he had just told the truth, we would have helped him through it, and only a few people would know," she said, frustration showing in her voice. "Now the whole world knows.

"Both my son and daughter were adopted as infants," Thelma told the court, now switching gears into a more biographical narrative. "I still remember picking her up from the adoption agency in L.A.

"My hopes and dreams for Lori are just gone, my

grandchildren are gone, and so is the joy that the grand-child would have brought to me, and to Lori.

"I will no longer be able to share recipes with Lori, meet her for lunch or a concert, shop for birthday or Christmas, no more e-mails or phone calls. I will never again hear her tell me 'Happy Mother's Day,' or 'I love you.' The list is endless.

"There is now an enormous vacuum, a hole in my being, and a rock has taken its place. Her friends, her room, are all reminders of her. I miss Lori so much. I mourn for her every minute. I frequently visit her grave.

"I am grateful that God allowed me to have and love Lori for even as long as I did. Only my faith has helped me through this."

And now, Thelma Soares told the court of the final insult that Mark Hacking had heaped upon her.

"I have been thrust onto the world stage, going from a quiet private life to celebrity. People recognize me. Some point and whisper, or strangers come and tell me that they are sorry for my loss."

Thelma related how intrusive the media had been throughout the ordeal.

"The media has jammed my phone line even though it was a private number," she said. "I have had to cover up the address numbers on my house. Before the last pre-trial another reporter from a local TV station showed up at my door with a satellite truck outside. There is always another article in the newspaper or magazine.

"I have had people from every state and sixty-three foreign countries and Antarctica contact me to tell me they were worried and prayed for Lori and me and the Hackings, and to tell me the impact Lori had on their lives."

Thelma told the court that complete strangers had sent her gifts, sheet music, DVDs, videos, paintings, butterflies, and ceramics.

"For months I could not sleep. I have used up all my sick leave, and at age sixty-seven, I need to have that sick leave. Every day this year, Mother's Day, Lori's birthday, her adoption day, have been so hard. There is a dark cloud that doesn't dissipate. I used to be a musical director at church and I loved it, but I couldn't even do one line of one song without bursting into tears. It has only been in the last week or two that I have begun to enjoy music again in a limited way."

It was now time for the confrontation that everyone in the room knew was coming.

"Mark called me at work to tell me that Lori had gone jogging and hadn't come home," she began. "I went to their apartment and stood within feet of where, hours earlier, he had killed Lori and put her in garbage bags."

The mother of Lori Hacking now turned to face Mark with the cold stare of one who has been driven beyond endurance.

"How could you do that, Mark? How could you do that to me?"

"Sorry," Mark said quietly.

She was finished.

Eraldo Soares walked to the podium with quiet dignity. The 71-year-old retired Spanish teacher from Farmdale, California, began by thanking the cops who had become such a part of his life during the weeks of searching for his daughter. He stood erect, wearing a long-sleeved white shirt with small dark stripes and a maroon print tie. The couple had called Lori their "Angel Baby" when they first got her from the LDS adoption agency in Los Angeles. They had waited seven years for a child.

Eraldo told of his daughter's 13-year-old birth mother, who had chosen to have her baby, then give her up for adoption. He called her selfless and told how she had sacrificed.

The father of Lori Hacking didn't wait long though to launch into his attack on the man who'd killed his Angel Baby, Mark Hacking.

"All we know of what happened is a statement from a known liar and perpetrator," he began.

"Did Lori confront him about his lies that night?" Eraldo asked.

"Did she suffer?" he continued. "Every time I see a garbage truck I wonder, did she have any life left in her while she was being compressed in the truck?"

Eraldo Soares told the court how he and his brother from Brazil had filled a vase with flowers and had taken the ceramic container to the landfill.

Again, tears began to flow from the eyes of courtroom observers, eyes barely dry from Thelma Soares' speech.

As her father spoke, observers witnessed the life force of this robust man ebb, slipping slowly from him as he described the joys of rearing their Angel Baby in childhood, then proudly watching her grow into an accomplished adult. Yet ebb it did, as Eraldo told of how his daughter was violated.

He told of how he had been taken to the spot where Lori was found. Then anger and grief overwhelmed him as he turned to Mark and began pounding the podium, saying, "Mark, how could you do that to my daughter?"

Eraldo told his son-in-law that he wanted him to rot away in his cell.

"You had a thing of beauty and you destroyed it," the Brazilian-American said in anger barely controlled.

Now Eraldo's words gripped the very gut of every man who has ever been divorced and separated from his children, saying how it had hurt to see Lori move to Utah with her mother.

"I actually lost Lori twice," he said.

Eraldo told the court how after the move, he would make the long drive across the desert in his VW bug, sometimes through blizzards, to see his daughter. When Lori would fly to California to see him, he would go to the airport an hour-and-a-half early just to meet her plane, and he would count every minute until she came. When it was time to go, he would walk her to the plane, and when Lori disappeared inside, his heart would break knowing that she was returning to Utah.

Finally, Eraldo Soares asked the court to keep Mark Hacking in prison for a long time as a message to future men who would kill their wives as they slept.

"Make the punishment fit the crime," he begged the judge.

When he sat down, Eraldo Soares wiped his eyes.

He had said what he needed to say. He would never speak to Mark again.

Mark Hacking almost looked forward to the speech he was virtually certain to hear from the judge as she pronounced his 6-years-to-life sentence. For months, he had dreaded this day, not because of the certainty that he would be spending much of his life in prison, but because of the certainty of facing his family in a public setting, and worse, facing the family of the woman he had killed and tossed aside.

"This is a sobering time for me," Judge Lindberg began as Mark, Gilbert Athay, and a lone deputy stood before her.

"I have read a voluminous pre-sentence report and many letters from Mark and his family. My words can't begin to lessen the pain each of you must feel. I hope this opportunity begins to help what will be a lifelong road to healing. Each letter and speech today has touched my heart. I'm still not sure who Mark Hacking is. I'm not sure Mark knows . . . Mark is a poster boy for dishonesty."

Mark Hacking had woven an intricate web of lies, and now Lindberg spoke of them and the "evil act of murdering Lori." She reviewed the methodical steps Hacking had taken to conceal the evidence, including depositing items in five different Dumpsters.

"He used the trust and good will of the community and nation seeking help for a missing wife. His alleged suicide attempt and more lies were another way to try and escape responsibility for what he has done.

"Look at what he put Lori, his family, and the

community through, then two months and thousands of hours of grueling work to recover some of Lori's remains.

"His dishonesty has cost two lives, and he also ruined his own life," she continued.

Lindberg addressed Mark Hacking, contempt in her voice.

"You have no one but yourself to blame," she said. "I sentence you to five years to life, with one additional year added because you used a firearm."

The judge then assessed a fine of $10,000, plus $120,672.12 in restitution for the cost of the search, recovery of Lori's remains, and victim restitution fund repayment.

Lindberg told the man standing before her that she hoped he served a very long period of time before he was even considered for release by the parole board.

To the east of the courthouse the Wasatch Mountains stood mute and gray as Mark Hacking was marched off into obscurity by six deputies. At a news conference in the rotunda, the major players in the case came again before the cameras for a final curtain call before they too returned to the anonymity of being nothing more than faces in a crowd.

More important things were happening in Zion as its citizens drove home in the 5 o'clock rush-hour traffic. It was raining again, and within days the Great Salt Lake would rise four feet.

Yet one mystery remained unsolved in the Lori Hacking murder case. When her body was found, according to the autopsy report curiously sealed from public scrutiny by Utah authorities, Lori Hacking was wearing jogging clothes.

She would never have gone to bed that way, according to those closest to her, but instead, being a devout Mormon, would have worn her garments.

That he had dressed his wife before he dumped her body was Mark Hacking's final lie—and nobody caught it.